Natural Crafts

Natural Crafts

72 Easy Projects

Marilyn Tower Oliver

Illustrations by Anna Rheee

STACKPOLE
BOOKS

Published by
STACKPOLE BOOKS
5067 Ritter Road
Mechanicsburg, PA 17055

Printed in the United States of America

First Edition

10 9 8 7 6 5 4 3 2 1

Cover design by Mark Olszewski
Cover art and interior illustrations by Anna Rheee
Photographs by Marilyn Tower Oliver

To Scott and Lauren, my creative kids, who as young children
inspired many of the craft projects in this book;

and to my mother, Ruth Scott Tower,
who always could see possibilities in the humble.

Library of Congress Cataloging-in-Publication Data

Oliver, Marilyn Tower.
    Natural crafts : 72 easy projects / Marilyn Tower Oliver : illustrations by Anna Rheee.—1st ed.
        p.   cm.
    ISBN 0-8117-2564-2
    1. Nature craft.   I. Title
TT157.O47   1994
745.5—dc20   94-7916
                                                                               CIP

Contents

Sand, Seashells, Stones, and Crystals

For Parents and Other Adults

There are two activities that almost every kid enjoys: exploring the outdoors and making things. Making crafts from natural materials satisfies both of these passions. This book offers a variety of crafts using natural materials that are readily available wherever you live. The projects range from those simple enough for a four- or five-year-old to more complex projects that may call for a parent's assistance. Many are suitable for use with youth groups, such as scouts or church schools. Adult supervision is necessary in crafts that involve heat, the stove, knives, or any other potentially dangerous items or activities, such as melting paraffin or wax.

Children are excited by everything they discover in nature—the variety of leaf shapes, the beauty of rocks and flowers, the colors of the sunset, patterns of light and shadow. Adults who share these wonders with children renew their own sense of awe at the marvels and ways of nature. And children who learn to appreciate nature when they are young are more likely to take an active role in protecting the environment when they become adults.

Making crafts helps the child develop manual dexterity, originality, and an awareness of texture, color, and form. Because originality should be nurtured and developed, these projects are designed to bring out the creativity of each child. In a group setting, each child's project will mirror his or her individuality, unlike art projects made from kits, whose results are all alike.

Creativity and intelligence are attributes most parents would like to foster in their children. Children are at their most creative when they are spontaneous and unconventional. In arts and crafts, creativity is unleashed when the artist is allowed to use his or her own ingenuity. The crafts in this book contain step-by-step directions, but these should be viewed as suggestions rather than rules. Use them as guides to get started, but feel free to experiment in order to create your own unique interpretations. Allow your child the freedom to be creative, to use a material differently.

One of the beauties of working with natural materials is their variety. No two feathers, stones, leaves, or flowers are identical. And because all natural materials vary, each interpretation will be slightly different.

Children thrive when adults take the time to share ideas, enthusiasm, and interests. Working together on craft projects is a good way to interact with children. Adults must be careful, however, not to compare children's work. Criticism stifles creativity. Making crafts should be fun, and it is an activity at which all may excel. There should be no fear of failure.

Artisans from many cultures have used natural materials to create objects of beauty. Take your child to craft exhibitions in museums and galleries so that he or she can see how natural materials have been used in various crafts.

Although it is all right to be messy while you are making a craft, cleanup is a necessary task that should be shared by all. Children should be encouraged to protect work surfaces with old newspapers, to clean brushes of paint or glue, and to return a work area to its neat state when the project is completed. If everyone helps, cleanup can be fun.

Above all, have fun when you use crafts to enjoy nature with your child. There is much to learn and much to delight both of you.

Rules for Safe Crafting

Crafting with objects from nature should be fun. Read and follow these rules to make sure that people and projects remain safe.

• Always read directions and cautions on the containers of such products as glue, paint, and paint thinner, and follow what they say.

• When using knives and other sharp tools, cut away from the body.

• Supervise small children when using knives, heat, fire, the stove, an iron, glue, spray paint, or any other potentially dangerous object or substance.

• Always melt wax or paraffin in a double boiler or in a coffee can or smaller pan set into a larger pan of water.

• Do not leave the stove unattended when you heat wax or paraffin.

• Do not work too quickly. Let paint and glue dry thoroughly before continuing to the next step.

• Keep your work area tidy so that you won't damage your project with smudges of paint or glue.

• Do not crowd your work area. Each artist must have sufficient room to work.

• Dispose of all products in a way that will not harm the environment, following the manufacturer's directions on the label.

• Do not pour extra plaster of paris down the sink, as it will stop up the drain. Dispose of it in the trash.

Gathering and Storing Materials

Part of the fun of nature crafting is gathering materials for your projects. Though you can buy some materials at craft stores and the supermarket, many crafts make use of objects that you will find on walks, at a lake or the seashore, or in your own backyard. Pine cones, pebbles, flowers, leaves, twigs, and sand are free for the taking. Soon you will develop an eye for unusual shapes, objects, and forms.

As you stroll along the beach, you will discover many treasures—seashells, bits of driftwood, bits of glass and pebbles tossed smooth by the motion of the sea. A walk in the park will provide colorful leaves, feathers, seedpods, and twigs. A hike in the woods or mountains will yield pine cones, grasses, interesting dry weeds, and bark from fallen trees or branches.

As a nature crafter, you should make an ongoing collection of treasures so that at any time of the year you will have materials on hand for a project. You can store these objects in paper bags or shoe boxes in the basement, garage, workroom, or a closet.

While you are making crafts from nature, it is important that you not have a negative impact on the environment. Here are some guidelines.

• Gather from living plants only what you need. Leave some for nature.

• Do not remove bark from a living tree. Use bark from fallen branches or trees or the bark that has fallen from the tree.

• Don't pull up entire plants with roots.

• Pick flowers in a way that does not injure the plant.

• Do not pluck feathers from living birds. Look for feathers on the ground.

• When you are gathering plant materials, do not trample flower gardens or fields.

• Always ask permission before you wander onto private property. Once you get permission to gather supplies, take only what you can use.

• Heed restrictions on your activities. In many parks and in all national forests, it is illegal to pick flowers, remove plants, peel bark from trees, or tamper with nature in any way.

• Be aware that some plants and flowers are endangered and must not be picked or removed from their natural growing place or habitat.

• Reuse and recycle whenever you can.

In addition to the materials and objects you can gather from nature, many natural materials—both ordinary and unusual—can be purchased inexpensively at supermarkets, art-supply or craft-supply stores, museums, and specialty stores. Corn husks, dried beans, lentils, spices, and bird seed can be found at supermarkets. Clay, which can be dug in many parts of the country, can be bought at craft-supply stores. In the fall, dried corn and gourds can be purchased to add to the dried flowers and weeds that you find for a Thanksgiving or autumn arrangement. Crystals, geodes, and gemstones can be found at museum gift shops, mineral stores, and at gem and mineral shows. Seashells can often be purchased at seaside resorts.

You can even find craft supplies in kitchen trimmings. Snips of carrots, radishes, or turnips are used for one project, and seeds from melons and pumpkins are used for mosaics or decorations on gift and place cards. Seeds from foods we eat can produce such houseplants as avocado trees and sweet potato vines.

Clippings from vines, shrubs, and trees can be used to make wreaths, baskets, and fiber weavings; dried foliage from flowering bulbs can be substituted for raffia in weaving baskets.

Making crafts with natural materials will spark the realization that the earth is a precious resource that should be appreciated and protected by young and old alike. It is our responsibility to see that the people who live here years from now will be able to enjoy the beauty of the outdoors and share a healthy environment with all the creatures that inhabit our planet.

Basic Tools and Materials

Most of the projects presented in this book can be made without special tools and equipment. Many of the tools you need will be found around the house. A few special materials can be purchased at an art-supply, craft-supply, or hardware store or at a florist's shop. Here is a list of some basic tools and materials to get you started.

Scissors
Screwdrivers
Pliers
Hammers
Files
Tweezers
Ruler
Pencils
Colored plastic tape
Masking tape
Scraps of wire
Wire coat hangers
Decorative adhesive paper
Waxed paper
Small brushes of assorted sizes
Toothpicks or wooden skewers
Low-fire clay
Florist's foam (porous material to support plants and flowers in arrangements)
Scraps of yarn, fabric, and ribbon
Plaster of paris
Spray paint
Acrylic paint
Tempera paint
Watercolors
Crayons and markers
Food coloring
Fabric dye
Fimo (a modeling dough that is hardened in the oven)
Rubber bands
Scraps of window glass
Paraffin
Strong nylon thread or dental floss
Needles and pins
Sandpaper
Silica gel, corn flour, or cat box litter
Sand
Newspaper
Colored paper
Shoeboxes or old gift boxes
Paper cups
Empty coffee cans and yogurt containers

Working with Plaster of Paris

Plaster of paris can be used to make many interesting and beautiful objects. It is inexpensive and easily found in hardware and craft stores.

Plan your project before you mix the plaster of paris with water. It is important to mix only as much plaster as you can use in twenty minutes, as it hardens quickly.

For sand casting, use a bucket or box one-half to two-thirds full of sand. Pour a small amount of water into the sand to moisten it. Make a form or cavity in the sand with your hands or a jar, bowl, or drinking glass. Smooth the sides of the form.

For small projects, measure ½ cup water into a clean, disposable container, such as an old yogurt container, milk carton, or coffee can. Add 1 cup of plaster of paris, and mix thoroughly with an old spoon or stick. The consistency should be that of yogurt or pancake batter. If the mixture looks too thin, add a little more of the powdered plaster; if too thick, add more water.

Pour the mixture into the cavity in the moistened sand. Add shells, rocks, or other ornamentation. Use a stick, nail, or pencil to make a hole for hanging the object, if desired. To keep this item from hardening into the plaster, jiggle it a little from time to time as the plaster cures.

Wait a couple of hours until the plaster of paris has cured before lifting the object from the sand.

Seeds

To own a bit of ground, to scratch it with a hoe, to plant seeds and watch the renewal of life—this is the commonest delight of the race, the most satisfactory thing a man can do.

—Charles Dudley Warner

Seeds are one of the basic building blocks of nature. Within the seed are the ingredients that determine what kind of plant it will become.

Seeds come in many sizes, some so small you can barely see them, and others, such as coconuts, very large. Nuts are a kind of seed, as are the pits of peaches, apricots, and avocados.

The projects in this section will enable you to see how seeds sprout into plants and to use your imagination in creating objects and jewelry decorated with seeds.

1. Potato Head

Small seeds can change their form quickly when they are planted and then carefully tended. Observing the process that transforms a seed into a plant is exciting. For this project you can use any kind of grass seed, but rye sprouts easily and quickly. If you want your potato head to have curly hair, use chia seeds instead.

Transforming a potato into a funny head with grass hair takes less than a week. The potato's face can be happy or sad, funny or serious. It's all up to the crafter.

Materials
- Large russet or baking potato
- Small amount of rye or other grass seed
- Flat saucer
- Teaspoon
- Toothpicks
- Cotton balls
- Buttons
- Snips of carrots, radishes, or turnips

Step 1.
Decide which end of the potato will be the bottom, then cut off both ends, making sure the bottom is level. With a spoon, scoop out 1 or 2 teaspoons of pulp from the top of the potato. Moisten the cotton balls and stuff them into the hole. Use enough to fill the hole completely.

Step 2.
Generously sprinkle the grass seed onto the wet cotton. Stand the potato on its bottom end in the saucer. Water the cotton several times a day, taking care not to wash away the seeds. A laundry sprinkling bottle or spray bottle will water gently. In a few days you will see that the seeds are begin-

ning to change. Soon a little green will appear. When the grass is about ½ inch high, it's time to give the potato head a face.

Step 3.
Using small pieces of broken toothpicks, attach buttons for eyes and snips of carrots, radishes, or turnips for nose and mouth. You can give the potato head a happy, sad, or goofy face. To keep the grass growing for a longer time, give a "haircut" when the grass reaches a length of several inches and keep the cotton moist.

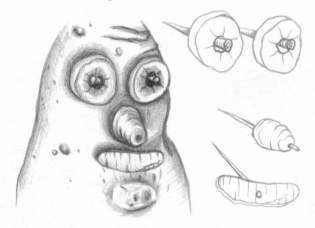

2. Sprouts to Eat

Sprouts from several kinds of seeds, such as alfalfa and mung beans, are delicious to eat as snacks or in sandwiches and salads; they are good sources of vitamins A and C plus many minerals. You can store them for about a week in the refrigerator either in a plastic bag or in a jar.

Sprouts are easy to grow at home using seeds from the health food store. Although alfalfa seeds are the most common, you will also find unusual combinations of seeds, many of which produce zesty sprouts. Be sure to use seeds that have not been treated with chemicals or fungicides for garden use.

Materials

Seeds for sprouts

Large wide-mouth canning jar made of clear glass, and canning band.

6-inch square of clean cheesecloth or a piece of window screen cut to fit inside the canning jar band

Strong rubber band

Large bowl

Strainer or colander

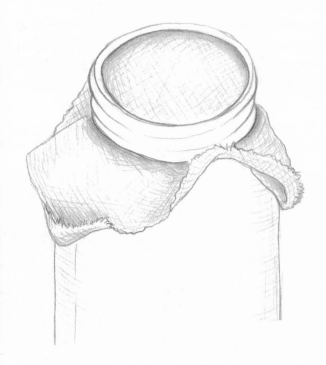

Step 1.
Place two or three tablespoons of seeds in the jar. Line the band with window screen, then screw it onto the jar, or else secure the cheesecloth over the mouth of the jar using a rubber band.

Step 2.
Fill the jar half full with lukewarm water. Soak the seeds overnight.

Step 3.
In the morning, drain the seeds and rinse several times with cool water. The cheesecloth or the lid fitted with screen will allow you to rinse without losing the seeds. Water left in the jar may cause the seeds to rot, so shake out every bit of water.

Step 4.
Lay the jar on its side out of direct sunlight, and keep it like that, rinsing the seeds several times a day, until they are ready to eat.

Step 5.
Once the sprouts have grown large enough to eat, remove the husks by carefully placing the sprouts in a large bowl. Fill the bowl with cool water. Scoop off the husks that rise to the top. Rinse and drain the sprouts several times through the strainer.

3. Seed Mosaic Picture

A mosaic is a picture made by arranging small pieces of colored glass, tiles, small stones, or other materials in a pattern. The craft is an ancient one. Centuries ago, the Romans made mosaic floors out of tiny stones placed in intricate designs.

Mosaics using seeds are easy to make and challenge the crafter's imagination. The most effective pictures are simple and use only a few shapes. They may show a scene from nature, such as flowers, fish, or leaves, or they may be abstract designs of circles, lines, squares, and triangles. Seed mosaics may be made on cardboard or on plywood. The following directions are for a mosaic on cardboard with its own frame. If you use plywood, drill holes for the yarn or string hanger.

Materials
   Cardboard lid from a shoebox or gift box
   White glue
   Paint brushes: 1-inch flat brush and a smaller, pointed watercolor brush

Tempera paint
Assorted dried beans, other seeds, and rice
Old newspapers
Yarn or string, 3 to 5 inches long
Old ballpoint pen or other pointed object
Scissors

about 1 inch apart in the lid, using the tip of an old ballpoint pen or another pointed object. Thread the string or yarn through the holes to use as a hanger, with the ends of the string on the back side of the lid. Knot each end and clip off excess.

Step 1.

First, protect your work surface with old newspaper. Then, using the 1-inch brush, paint the inside of the box lid with tempera paint and allow the paint to dry. Rinse the paint from your brush.

Step 2.

Plan your design. You can sketch the design on a piece of scratch paper as a guide. Simple shapes work best.

Step 3.

When the paint is dry, poke two small holes

Step 4.

With the pencil, lightly draw the outline of your design in the lid. Then use the smaller brush to fill in one shape with white glue. It is best to work from the top down. Sprinkle one kind of seed thickly over the glue, using the pen to press the seeds into the glue. Go on to the second shape, this time using another kind of seed. Continue in this manner until you have completed your picture. It is not necessary to completely cover the box lid with seeds; leaving some areas of the background exposed will provide contrast and enhance the design. Let the seeds dry, then make sure they are all firmly attached. If any are loose, paint over them with diluted white glue, one part glue to two parts water, then rinse the glue from your brush. Avoid the painted areas.

4. Seed Plaques

You can make a round plaque with mosaics of dried beans and seeds that can be hung in a window or placed on a table. Use several small plaques to make a mobile. Seeds that are attractive for this craft include small black beans, kidney beans, striped pinto beans, yellow and green split peas, lentils, and bird seed. Enjoy the differences in texture and color created by using a variety of seeds.

Materials
- Assorted dried beans and other seeds
- Several plastic margarine or coffee can lids
- White glue
- Yarn
- Small brush
- Small disposable container
- Old newspapers
- Pencil
- Fishing line or nylon filament
- Scissors

Step 1.

Protect your work surface with old newspapers. Using the small brush, coat a plastic lid with white glue.

Step 2.

Use one type of seed to outline the border of the lid.

Step 3.

Press other beans and seeds into the glue, arranging them in a simple design. You can use the tip of a pencil to position them. Work with one kind of bean or seed at a time. When your design is complete, mix one part white glue and two or three parts water, and brush this over the beans and seeds.

Step 4.

Place the lid in a warm, dry place and allow the glue to dry completely. This may take several hours.

Step 5.

With the small brush, paint white glue around the outer edge of the lid. Cut a length of yarn that is about twice the circumference of the lid. Press the yarn around the edge to make a frame, and use the ends to tie a bow at the top. Allow the glue to dry thoroughly.

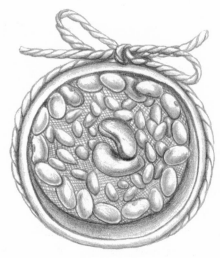

Step 6.

To hang the plaque, thread a length of nylon line through the bow and knot the ends.

5. Seed Pincushion

A seed-decorated pincushion makes a practical Mother's Day gift. This project makes use of articles that are usually discarded. Bottles of vitamins and other pills come packed with cotton, which can be recycled for this project; several bottles will provide enough cotton for a pincushion.

You may want to experiment using materials other than seeds, such as small shells or pebbles, to decorate your pincushion.

Materials

Lid from a spray can, or a clean cat food or tuna can with label removed

Fabric scrap about 5 inches square for the lid, 6 inches square for a can

Seeds, dried beans, rice, lentils, or small seashells or pebbles

White glue

Latex or enamel spray paint

Paint thinner for cleanup or enamel paint

String or strong thread

Cotton or fiberfill

Paintbrush, ½ to 1 inch wide

Step 1.
Cover your work surface with old newspaper. With the brush, coat the outside of the can or lid with white glue. Rinse your brush.

Step 2.
Pour about ½ cup of the seeds, beans, lentils, rice, shells, or pebbles on the newspaper. Roll the glue-covered outside surface of the can over the seeds or other material. Cover the surface as thickly as possible. Allow the glue to dry several hours or overnight, until the seeds or other material is firmly in place.

Step 3.

Paint the outside of the can. Do this outdoors, where there is good ventilation. (Young children will need to be supervised.) Clean your brush. Let the paint dry.

Step 4.

Stuff the can with cotton or fiberfill to determine how much you will need for the pincushion. The filling should puff slightly at the top and be firm enough to hold pins. Take the filling out and shape it into a ball.

Step 5.

Place the fabric scrap on the table, right side down. Put the ball of filling in the middle of the fabric, gather the edges up, and tie securely with string or strong thread, doubled.

Step 6.

Cover the bottom and inner sides of the can with a small quantity of white glue. Place the ball of cotton and cloth into the can, tied end down. Let the glue dry, and your pincushion is ready to hold needles and pins.

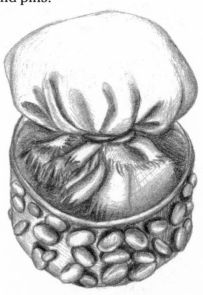

6. Bird Seed Mystery Garden

A package of mixed bird seed can hold many surprises. It may contain grain sorghum, a type of tropical cereal that is used to make syrup; millet, a grain mentioned in the Bible; and sunflower seeds, which can produce tall plants with enormous flowers. You can add to this mixture a pinch of rye grass seed, a few lentils, and some seeds left over from a summer melon or a Halloween pumpkin. Sprinkle the seeds in a pot filled with potting soil, and watch the seeds quickly germinate to create an unusual planter.

Seeds that germinate quickly often produce plants that do not live long. As the plants in your bird seed garden die out, you can reseed the flowerpot for more greenery. You may also want to plant several of the seedlings in the garden. One may grow into a giant sunflower.

Materials
Mixed bird seed
Potting soil
Flowerpot or other container
Liquid plant food

Step 1.
If there is a drainage hole in the bottom of the container, cover it with a pebble or a piece of broken flowerpot. Place the potting soil in the container, and moisten.

Step 2.
Sprinkle the seed mixture generously over the soil, then cover with a thin layer of soil. Keep the soil moist but not soggy. Do not overwater.

Step 3.
In about a week you will see the seeds beginning to sprout.

Apply a weak solution of liquid fertilizer every other week.

7. Aromatic Spice Necklace

Many spices come from seeds, berries, and buds that have delightful aromas. Whole spices may be used to make a necklace that gives off a natural perfume. The necklace may be worn as jewelry, or it can be placed in a drawer to freshen clothes or linens. If you make a short necklace—one that doesn't slip over your head—add ribbon ties as a fastener.

Allspice and cloves have pungent, spicy fragrances. Allspice comes from the berry of a tree that grows in the West, and cloves are the dried buds of a tropical tree. Often these spices are ground into powders for seasoning foods. Be sure to get whole cloves or allspice for this project; these can be found at the grocery store.

Materials
    Whole cloves or allspice
    Bowl of water
    Strong thread
    Needle
    Narrow ribbon or thick yarn, 12 inches long
(optional)
    Scissors

Step 1.

Soften the cloves or allspice by soaking it overnight in a bowl of water. Then drain off the water.

Step 2.

Cut the thread to the desired length of the finished necklace plus 10 extra inches. Thread the needle.

Step 3.

String the softened, wet spices onto the thread, leaving about 4 inches at each end. You can use either cloves or allspice or mix the two. If you use cloves, pierce them through the stem just

below the ball. Fit the spices closely together. Once you've finished stringing the spices, knot the ends several times. Then tie the ends together and clip off the excess thread. Allow the seeds to dry.

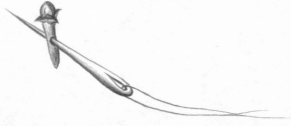

Step 4.

If you'd like to make a shorter necklace (one that you won't be able to slip over your head), sew ribbon or yarn to the ends after the seeds are strung, using the excess thread. Cut the ribbon in the center and trim off the extra thread. To wear the necklace, tie the ribbon or yard in a bow at the back.

8. Seedpod Necklace

In many parts of the world, people use seedpods to make lovely necklaces. You can use seedpods that you gather on a nature walk or dried beans purchased at the market. You can make a necklace that is long enough to slip over your head or a shorter one that ties with ribbons, and you can use one type of beans or seeds or mix several varieties.

Materials

Dried beans, seeds, or seedpods
Food color, fabric dye, or spray paint (optional)
Bowl of water
Strong thread
Needle
Scissors
Narrow ribbon, 12 inches long (optional)
Glue or clear nail polish

Step 3.

String the pods or beans on the thread, pushing them close together so that there are no gaps between them. It may take days or even several weeks for the pods to dry. Because green pods tend to shrink, you may have to continue pushing them together as they dry. You may add more pods if you wish.

Step 4.

When the pods are thoroughly dry, you can spray paint them gold or silver, or another color, if desired.

Step 5.

If your pod necklace is long enough to slip over your head, tie the ends in a strong knot. Clip off excess thread. Put a drop of glue or clear nail polish on each knot so the ends will not unravel.

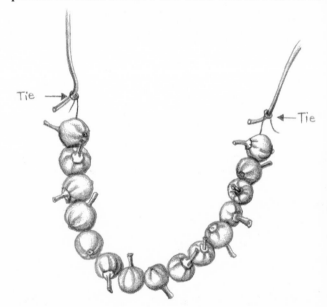

Step 1.

Soak dried beans in a bowl of water for several hours or overnight to soften them. If you want to color white beans, add food color or fabric dye to the water. Do not let the beans stand in the water for too long, as they may spoil. Soak seedpods if they are hard. Fresh, green pods may be strung without soaking.

Step 2.

Cut the thread to the desired length of the finished necklace plus 10 extra inches.

Step 6.

For a shorter necklace, cut the narrow ribbon in half. Tie or sew the ends of the ribbon to the necklace.

9. Seed Mosaic Gift Box
or Pencil Holder

S eeds mosaics can be used to decorate many different objects. You can transform a matchbox into a small gift box by covering it with bright construction paper and a seed design, or create a colorful pencil holder from an empty frozen juice container. For this project, you can use bird seed, lentils, split peas, rice, barley, melon seeds, or small seeds collected on a nature walk. For a group project, the leader may want to cut the construction paper to size in advance.

Materials

Empty box for kitchen matches, 2½ by 5 inches, or empty 12-ounce frozen juice container, washed and dried

Assorted small seeds, rice, lentils, barley, or split peas

Construction paper

White glue

Paper clips

Rubber bands

Pie or cake pan

Spoon

Old newspapers

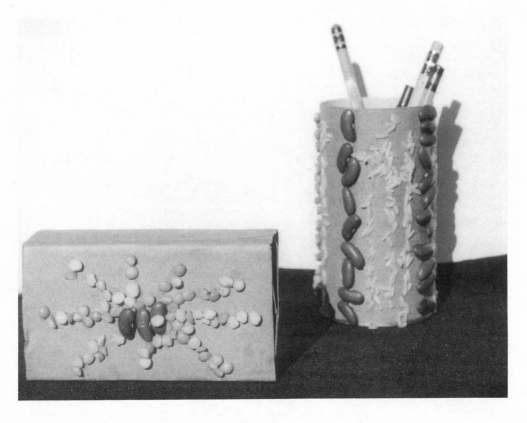

Step 1.
Cut construction paper 4¾ by 8½ inches to cover the matchbox, or 8½ by 5 inches to cover the juice can.

Step 2.
Spread glue evenly on one side of the paper. Carefully wrap the paper around the box or can. Use paper clips or rubber bands to secure the paper so that it will dry smoothly. Let dry.

Step 3.
Once the glue has dried, remove the clips or bands and plan a simple geometric design using triangles, stripes, or circles. With glue, paint one shape and then, holding the box over the pie or cake pan to

catch any extra seeds, spoon one kind of seed over the glue and press into the glue. Repeat for each shape with different seeds until you have completed the design. Allow the glue to dry completely.

10. Place Cards

Colorful place cards decorated with flowers made from seeds will beautify the table for a birthday party or special dinner or lunch.

Materials

    3-by-5-inch unlined index cards or 3-by-4-inch pieces of construction paper

    White glue

    Yellow split peas and rice, melon seeds, or green split peas

    Fine-point marker pen

Step 1.

Fold cards or construction paper in half lengthwise.

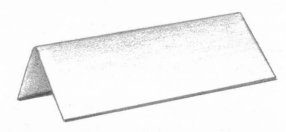

Step 2.

In the upper left-hand corner just below the fold, glue rice, melon seeds, or green split peas to represent flower petals. Glue a yellow split pea in the center of each flower. With a green marker pen, draw a stem and leaves. Write a guest's name on each card below the design.

11. Tie-Dyed Scarf
Using Dried Beans

The shapes of dried beans provide unique patterns in this tie-dye project. Garbanzo beans, or chickpeas, will produce a star shape; kidney beans will make an oval.

When you dye fabric, you also explore the world of color. Two colors will combine to make a third color: blue plus yellow makes green, red plus yellow produces orange, and red plus blue comes out purple.

After you have completed this scarf, you may want to tie-dye a cotton T-shirt.

Materials

12-inch square of white cotton muslin or sheeting (avoid synthetic fabrics)

2 packages of dye, one light color such as yellow or pink and a darker color such as deep blue

Salt, if called for in dye package instructions
Dry garbanzo and kidney beans
Rubber bands
Large pan
A second pan for transporting the cloth from the kettle to the sink
Spoon or tongs

Step 1.
Wash and iron the fabric to remove sizing or fillers. You can hem the square, or make a fringe by pulling out several threads along each side.

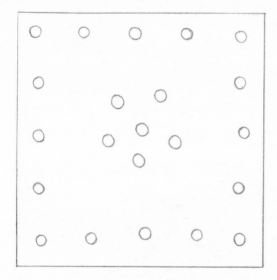

Step 2.
Starting in the center of the square, place a dried kidney or garbanzo bean on the fabric, and wrap a rubber band tightly around the bean eight to ten times. Continue placing beans in the fabric and tying them with the rubber bands. Every place you put a rubber band will remain white after the fabric is dyed.

Step 3.
Fill a large pan with hot water and bring it to a boil. (Supervise young children.) Dissolve the lighter-colored dye in a cup or two of water, then add to the boiling water, stirring to mix the color evenly. Wet the entire tied fabric in tap water, then place the fabric in the pot of water. The water should cover the cloth. Let the cloth boil gently for about 30 minutes, stirring occasionally. Using tongs, lift the fabric out of the water and place in a pan to catch excess water. Use caution, as the cloth will be hot. Rinse the cloth in cool tap water until the water runs clear. Squeeze to remove excess water. Do not remove the rubber bands. It is not necessary to dry the fabric before continuing with the next step.

Step 4.
Wrap a second rubber band behind the first; this will keep an area of color you have just dyed from absorbing the second color. If you wish, you may wrap more beans into the fabric at this time. These will make a design in a third color. To add variety to your pattern, you can place two rubber bands around some of the beans and leave one around others.

Step 5.
Prepare the second dye bath and dye the fabric until it is a shade darker than the hue you want. Again, rinse in cool water until the water runs clear.

Step 6.
For a smooth-textured scarf, remove the bands now, and press the scarf with a medium-hot iron when the fabric is almost dry. If you want an unusual bumpy texture, let the material completely dry before removing the rubber bands. This will produce a puckered texture, something like seersucker.

12. Sweet Potato Vine

Plants grow from roots and bulbs as well as from seeds. Some roots, such as potatoes and sweet potatoes, are edible. A sweet potato can be sprouted to make an attractive and unusual houseplant that will cost just pennies to grow. In a matter of a few weeks, you will see the root transform itself into a lush vine. A short time after you start your plant in a clear glass or jar, you will see roots begin to form. Soon green shoots will appear from the top of the sweet potato. Before you know it, you will need to transplant it to a larger container to give it more room to grow.

Materials
    Sweet potato
    4 to 6 toothpicks
    Clear glass or jar
    Flowerpot
    Potting soil

Step 1.
Push the toothpicks into the sweet potato about one-third up from the blunt or flatter end.

Step 2.

Place the flat end of the sweet potato in the glass or jar. The toothpicks will support the sweet potato so that only the bottom one-third is in water.

Step 3.

Pour water into the jar to cover the end. Place the jar in a window where it will receive light. Check the jar regularly to make sure that the end is still in water. Add water if necessary. In a week or two you will see roots growing from the bottom. Soon, green leaves will sprout from the top. In a short while, your sweet potato will have long vines with a purple tint. Keep water around the roots.

Step 4.

When the roots outgrow the jar, transplant your sweet potato vine to a flowerpot filled with potting soil.

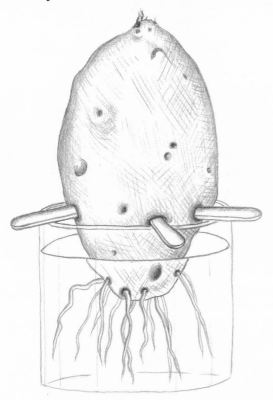

13. Avocados and Other Plants from Food

We often throw away food scraps and pits that can grow into interesting plants. Here are some you may want to try.

Avocados

Avocados can grow into large trees in the semi-tropical climates of California and Florida. The pit inside an avocado sprouts into a handsome plant with dark green foliage. To produce fruit, avocado seedlings usually have to be grafted onto an older tree, but even without fruit, the avocado is worth growing. In warm climate, the avocado plant may be grown outdoors, but where winters are cold, keep it indoors and pinch it back to keep it from growing too large.

Sometimes, when you cut open an avocado,

you will find a pit that has already begun to sprout. You can also grow a plant from a pit that has not sprouted, but you must first force it to sprout in water. As the pit sprouts, it will split and you will be able to see the small beginnings of a tree.

Materials

    Avocado pit
    Drinking glass or glass jar
    4 to 6 toothpicks
    Flowerpot
    Potting soil

Step 1.
Cut open an avocado and remove the pit. If any pulp sticks to the pit, wash it off.

Step 2.
Note that the pit has a pointed end and a flatter

end. With the pointed end up, stick toothpicks into the pit about one-third up from the flat end.

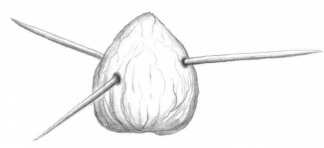

Step 3.
Place the pit in the mouth of the glass or jar with the flat end pointing down. The toothpicks will rest on the rim of the glass or jar and support the pit.

Step 4.
Pour water into the glass or jar until it touches the flat end of the pit. Keep the water at this level. You will have to wait patiently for several weeks until a root appears at the bottom of the pit. Soon the pit will begin to split.

Step 5.
Once roots have developed, plant the pit in potting soil. Water regularly; don't let the soil get soggy, but don't let it dry out completely. Soon your plant will appear. You may have to transplant it to a larger pot as it grows.

Step 6.
Fertilize weekly with citrus food.

Potatoes

Place a potato in a dry place to get it to sprout, then plant it in a large pot or in the garden. It will produce a plant with lacy leaves. After several months, poke around the roots. You may find tiny potatoes that you can cook.

Onions

Onions are bulbs that will produce handsome flowers. Plant onions that have sprouted in the garden with the green sprouts pointed upward. Eventually, the onion will produce a large, round flower that can be picked and added to a bouquet. An onion will sprout if left out in a dry place.

Carrot tops

Carrot tops sprout lacy leaves. Simply cut ½ to 1 inch from the tops and place the cut side down in a saucer of water. In a day or two green sprouts will appear. They will last about a week.

Tomatoes

If you bury a rotten tomato in a flowerpot or in the garden, you will soon have many small tomato plants. When they are several inches high, pick out the strongest-looking ones and transplant each into a large pot or into your garden about 1½ feet apart. Cherry tomatoes are especially easy to grow this way.

14. Fruit Pit Harvest Wreath

Pits and stones from summer fruits, such as peaches, apricots, nectarines, plums, and cherries, are seeds that can be used in craft projects. A unique wreath can be crafted from fruit pits. The size of the finished wreath will determine how many pits you will need. Use dried beans, lentils, or split peas as fillers. The browns and beiges of the fruit pits make this wreath, placed against a background of fall leaves, perfect for an autumn decoration. To transform the wreath into a table centerpiece, place a votive candle in the center and decorate the edges with evergreen boughs or colorful leaves.

Materials

Pits from peaches, apricots, nectarines, plums, or cherries
Dried beans, lentils, or split peas
Heavy cardboard, 8 by 8 inches
Bowl

Household bleach
Water
Heavy-duty white glue
Heavy scissors or X-acto knife
Pen or pencil
Compass, or bowl and glass

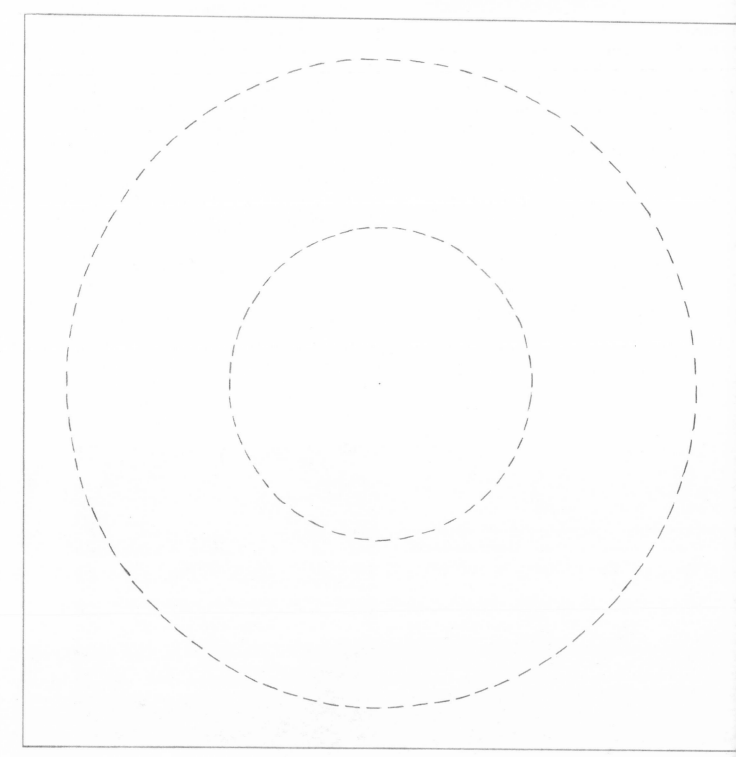

Step 1.

Collect pits from summer fruits until you have enough to make the wreath. Select dried beans or peas of a color you think looks good with the pits.

Step 2.

Soak the pits for a half hour in a solution made of half household bleach and half water. Remove the pits and allow them to dry for a day.

Step 3.

Arrange the pits on the cardboard in a wreath shape to determine how wide your wreath can be. Indicate the outer and inner circumferences with pen or pencil dots. Set the pits aside.

Step 4.

Use a compass and pencil to draw inner and outer circles on the cardboard. If you don't have a compass, use a bowl and a glass of the appropriate sizes and trace them with a pencil, following the pattern on the preceding page.

Step 5.

Cut the outer circle around the outline using scissors or an X-acto knife. Cut out the inner circle. (An adult should cut the wreath for young children. Older children should be supervised.)

Step 6.

Apply heavy-duty white glue to the cardboard. Arrange the pits on the cardboard, positioning the larger pits first. Fill in the empty spaces with smaller pits. If you don't have enough pits to completely cover the wreath, fill in the empty spaces with the beans, lentils, or split peas.

Step 7.

Allow the glue to dry thoroughly. To hang the wreath, glue a loop of string on the back.

15. Spring Basket with Natural Grass

This spring basket of rye grass can be used as an Easter basket, to capture the wonder of the spring season, or as a thoughtful gift for someone in a nursing home or hospital. If you wish, you may add decorated eggs or artificial or fresh flowers. In this project, a large plastic bag transforms your basket into a miniature greenhouse to aid in sprouting the seeds.

Materials

Basket

Rye grass seed

Plastic wrap

Dry cleaner's bag or other large, clear plastic bag

Vermiculite (available at a nursery or garden shop)

Rubber band

Step 1.
Completely line the basket with plastic wrap. It may be necessary to use two pieces; overlap them by several inches.

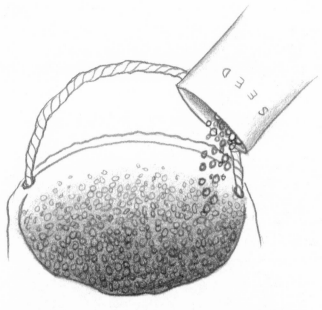

Step 4.
Place the basket in the plastic bag. Drape the plastic over the top of the basket handle and secure it with a rubber band. Put the basket in an out-of-the-way corner.

Step 2.
Fill the basket with vermiculite.

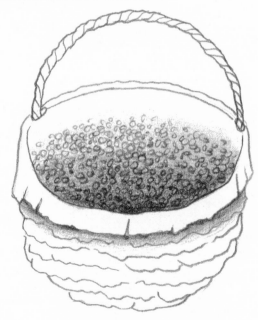

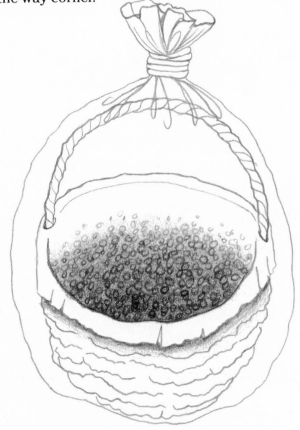

Step 3.
Sow the rye grass seed thickly over the vermiculite. Sprinkle the basket with water. Moisten thoroughly, but don't make the basket soggy.

Step 5.

Check daily to see whether the vermiculite is still moist. If it is dry, sprinkle with water.

Step 6.

When green shoots appear, remove the plastic covering and give the basket more light. Water the grass regularly. Within a few days, you will have a lush carpet of grass overflowing the basket.

Cones, Bark, and Feathers

Come, doves, that are mine now,
With feathers so fine now!

—Bjornsterne Bjornson

Nature has many coverings. Among them are cones and pods, which hold seeds; bark, a protective covering for trees; and feathers and fur, which provide animals with protection and warmth.

You can make many craft projects from bark, pine cones, and seedpods. Do not take them from living trees, however. Use cones, pods, and pieces of bark that you find lying on the ground, or take bark from branches or trees that have fallen. Pine cones can be found in almost every region, but they vary in size and shape. It isn't necessary to take a trip to the mountains to obtain cones and pods to use in crafts. Gather them on nature walks or, if you live in the city, in parks and along city streets. The fall is a particularly good time to look for them.

You can use almost any combination of seedpods and pine cones. Add feathers you have gathered on walks. Construction paper can be used for beaks, feathers, and ears; most craft and fabric shops carry eyes that you can glue to your creatures' faces; pipe cleaners, wire, or twigs can serve as legs and feet.

You can use pine cones and seedpods to create realistic or fanciful insects, birds, and animals.

Feathers and fur can also be used in many craft projects. You will be surprised at the variety of feathers you will find on the ground when you take nature walks. Birds molt, or shed feathers, to make way for new growth. You can also save the fur you comb from your dog or cat to weave into natural tapestries.

16. Bark-Covered Book

When you take a walk in the woods or in a park, look on the ground for large pieces of bark that some trees shed yearly. You can use these pieces of bark to cover a miniature handmade book that will make a special gift for a friend or a treasured keepsake.

The size of your book will depend on the bark that you gather. Our instructions are for a book that measures 3 by 3½ inches. Follow the same process for smaller or larger books. You may also want to make books using handmade or unusual paper rather than bark for the cover.

Materials

2 sheets of 8½-by-11-inch bond paper
Ruler
Pencil
Scissors
Needle and strong thread, or a large stapler
Cardboard, at least 4 by 6 inches
White glue
8 to 10 large paper clips
2 bark strips, each at least 2½ by 3½ inches
Decorative paper, cloth, or ribbon, 3 inches wide

Step 1.

Measure and cut the bond paper into five pieces, each 3½ by 6 inches.

Step 2.

Stack the papers one sheet on top of the other, then fold down the center so that you have a ten-page booklet measuring 3 by 3½ inches.

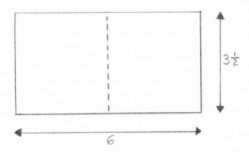

Step 3.

Thread the needle with double thread; knot the ends together securely.

Step 4.

Sew the pages of the booklet together, stitching down the center on the fold line. Turn and sew back up to the top of the booklet. Sew back and forth over the top of the booklet several times to secure the thread. Cut the extra thread neatly. Instead of sewing, you can staple the booklet along the center fold, with the ends of the staples pointing toward the outside of the fold.

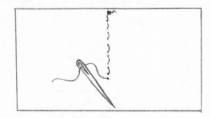

Step 5.

To make the covers of the book, measure and cut two 3-by-3½-inch pieces of cardboard.

Step 6.

Glue the cardboard pieces to the front and back pages of the booklet. To keep the remaining eight pages from touching the glue, paper-clip them together at sides and top to separate them from the covers. Allow the glue to dry.

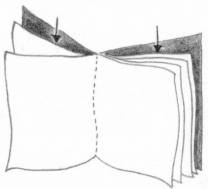

Step 7.

Cut two pieces of bark 2½ by 3½ inches. Glue the bark to the cardboard back and front of the booklet. Secure the bark with paper clips while the glue dries.

Step 8.

Trim the top, bottom, and opening sides of the booklet so that the cardboard does not show.

Step 9.

Measure a 3-by-3½-inch piece of decorative paper, wide ribbon, leather, or cloth to cover the outside fold of the book, called the spine. Glue the decorative spine to the outside fold, slightly overlapping the bark on the front and back of book, and allow it to dry thoroughly.

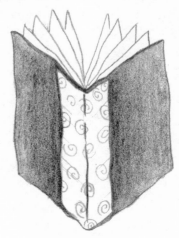

17. Corn Husk Pioneer Couple

In the past, when toys were not readily available, people had to make do with what they had on hand. Toys were whittled or carved from wood. Dolls were fashioned from corn husks, apples, and nuts. This corn husk couple recalls the days of the pioneers.

Materials
- Corn husks
- Heavy thread or string
- White glue
- Small twig
- Yarn or corn silk
- Scissors
- Bowl of warm water
- Towel

Step 1.

Soften the corn husks by soaking them in a bowl of warm water for ten minutes. Then lay them on a towel to absorb excess water.

Step 2.

Cut the string or heavy thread as follows: one piece 10 inches long; one piece 5 inches long; one piece 4 inches long; and four pieces 3 inches long.

Step 3.

Taking one medium-sized piece of corn husk, make a ball. This is the head.

Step 4.

To add the torso, take a triangular piece of corn husk, find the center, and fold it over the ball. The point of the husk is at the back of the head. To form the neck, place the triangular piece of husk in the center of the 10-inch piece of string. Wrap the string several times around. Tie at the back. You should have two tails of string that measure about 4 inches each. Carefully tear the lower section of the triangle in half lengthwise. Set aside.

Step 5.

Select a piece of corn husk to form the doll's arms. Fold the husk lengthwise. Tie a piece of 3-inch string near each end of the husk to indicate wrists. With scissors, trim each end bluntly below the string. Slip the arms between the front and back portions of the torso, pushing them up toward the neck. Take the strings tying the neck and crisscross them across the front of the torso. Bring to the back, cross, and return to the front, knotting securely.

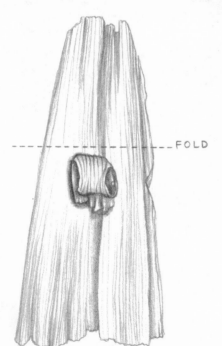

FOLD

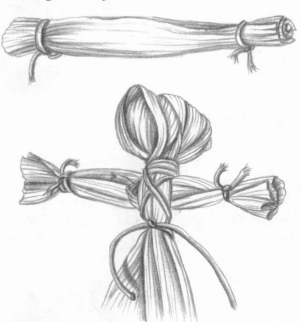

Step 6.

Form the woman's skirt by taking several pieces of husk and cutting them straight across the pointed end. Gather around the torso, wrap the 5-inch piece of string several times around the waist, and knot the string. Cut the bottom of the skirt evenly so that the doll will stand.

Step 8.

Glue yarn or corn silk on the dolls' heads for hair.

Step 9.

To make an apron for the woman, tie a shorter piece of corn husk over the skirt using the 4-inch-long string. Tie a narrow strip of corn husk over the string.

Step 7.

To make the man, follow steps 1 through 6, then cut the skirt evenly in half vertically. To form pant legs, tuck a narrower strip of husk under the string that secures the waist, then twist the husk around one skirt half. Repeat on the other side. Tie the ankles with 3-inch pieces of string. Clip the bottoms of the legs evenly so that the figure will stand.

Step 10.

Clip all string ends closely.

18. Fall Door Decoration

This door hanging, made from small ears of corn, is a wonderful way to welcome autumn visitors to your home. You can decorate your arrangement with ribbon or with strips of stiffened calico. (Fabric stiffener is available at fabric stores.)

Materials

3 or 4 small, dried ears of colorful Indian corn with husks

Florist's wire, 12 inches long

Ribbon or calico strip, approximately 1 yard long and 1¼ inch wide

Fabric stiffener (if using calico)

Scissors

Finish wrapping at the back of the arrangement, leaving at least 3 inches of wire at each end. Twist the ends together tightly several times to secure the corn. Make a loop out of the ends to form a hanger.

Step 1.

Arrange the corn so that the larger ears are to the back and the smallest ear is at the front. Wrap the florist's wire around the husks several times.

Step 2.

If you wish to make a calico ribbon, cut a yard-long strip of calico 1¼ inches wide. Rub the stiffener over the fabric. Hang the strip and allow to dry thoroughly.

Step 3.

Tie the ribbon or stiffened calico around the corn husks to cover the wire. Make a bow in the front. Cut a V in each end. Any extra ribbon can be pinned to the back of the arrangement. Clip ends in a V.

19. Pine Cone Bird Feeder

In the fall, many wild birds migrate south. A pine cone bird feeder will provide sustenance for them on their journey, as well as a treat for local birds that overwinter. You'll be surprised at the variety of birds that will stop by for food. Hang your feeder out of the reach of neighborhood cats.

Materials

    Medium to large pine cone
    Cord or yarn, 2 feet long
    Peanut butter
    Bird seed
    Dinner knife
    Hook or nail
    Pie or cake pan

Step 1.
Center the length of cord or yarn around the pine cone tip, and wrap around the tip several times. Leave about 8 inches of cord extending at each end. Tie a knot, then tie the two ends at the top to form a loop for hanging.

Step 2.
Spread peanut butter over the surface of the cone with the dinner knife, being sure to fill all the spaces and packing it tightly.

Step 3.
Sprinkle bird seed in the pie or cake pan. Roll the pine cone in the bird seed, then press the seeds into the peanut butter with the knife.

Step 4.
Hang the pine cone bird feeder on a tree branch or from the eaves.

20. Floating Walnut Shell Candles

Walnut shell candles floating in a shallow bowl of water make an attractive and unusual centerpiece. (For safety, do not leave the lit candles unattended.) The shells are broken in half and filled with melted paraffin or wax from old candles. As walnut shells do not always break evenly, you may have to crack more than three to four walnuts to get six to eight halves. Adults need to assist in making this project.

Materials

6 to 8 walnut shell halves

Knife

Hammer

1 block paraffin or 6 to 8 inches of used candles

Coffee can

Pan of water

Pot holder

Nail

Wick or heavy string, 8 inches long, cut into 1-inch pieces

Shallow bowl of water

Step 1.

Break the walnuts in half by inserting the knife blade in the crack at the top of the shell. Hit the top of the knife with the hammer to crack the shell open. Dig out the nut meat and set aside to eat later.

Step 2.

Place the paraffin or candles in the coffee can, and set the can in a pan of water. Heat the water and melt the wax. Do not leave the stove while you are melting the wax, as it can easily ignite.

Step 3.

Once the wax has melted, remove the pan from the heat. Using the pot holder, lift the can out of the water. Carefully pour melted wax into each walnut half. Reserve a small quantity of wax to use later for securing the wicks.

Step 4.

Allow the wax to cool in the shells ten to fifteen minutes, until it is slightly firm. Then use the nail to poke a hole into the center of the wax in each shell. Insert a piece of wick in each hole.

Step 5.

Reheat the wax you have reserved. Pour a small quantity into each shell to secure the wick, and allow to harden.

Step 6.

Pour several inches of water into a shallow bowl. Float the candles in the water, and light them carefully. Do not leave them unattended.

21. Feather Earrings

Unusual jewelry using natural materials is easy and inexpensive to make. Feathers and beads combine to make these earrings with a Native American flavor. You can get the earring findings at a craft or jewelry-supply store.

Materials
   Earring findings
   Needle-nose pliers
   Wire cutters or scissors
   2 or 4 small, decorative feathers
   Thin brass wire, 3 inches long
   2 small beads
   White glue

Step 1.
Jam the pointed ends of one or two feathers into the holes of each bead. Secure with a drop of glue.

Step 2.
Cut two pieces of wire, each about 1½ inches long.

Step 3.
Using needle-nose pliers, make a small loop at the end of each piece of wire.

Step 4.

Push the straight end of one piece of wire up through the hole of one bead, starting from the side with the feather. Pull through the bead carefully so as not to bend the feathers. The loop at the end will secure the wire in the bead. Repeat with the other bead.

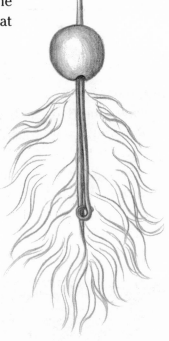

Step 5.

Wrap the straight end of the wire around the loop of the earring finding. Twist several times, and clip off the excess wire. Repeat for the other earring.

22. Pine Cone and Seedpod Turkey

This turkey, made from a pine cone and a seed-pod from a sweet gum tree, will grace your Thanksgiving table.

Materials

Pine cone, 5 to 6 inches long

Red and orange construction paper

8 to 10 chicken or other feathers

Sweet gum pod (or other round seedpod about 1 inch in diameter)

Heavy black or brown pipe cleaner

Scissors

White glue

Step 1.

Lay the pine cone on its side. The pointed end will be the front end of the turkey.

Step 2.

Outline tail feathers on the red and the orange construction paper. (See pattern above.) Cut the tail pieces out and glue together at base. Glue these to the flat end of the cone. Allow to dry.

Step 3.

Measure and cut the pipe cleaner to 7 inches. Twist one end two or three times around the pointed tip of the pine cone.

Step 4.

Pull the other end of the pipe cleaner up to make a long neck, and glue into one of the holes in the sweet gum pod. This forms the head.

Step 5.

Outline the beak on a piece of construction paper. Cut out and glue to the front of the head.

Step 6.

Dip the ends of the real feathers in white glue, and position them between the end of the pine cone and the construction-paper tail feathers.

23. Pine Cone Owl

This wise old owl is made from two pine cones. Display him on a forked tree branch. If you can't find cones in the sizes indicated, you can use smaller ones.

Materials

2 pine cones, one 4 inches and one 3 inches long

2 purchased eyes

Construction paper (yellow or orange)

Glue

Medium-gauge wire, 5 inches long

Forked branch

Step 1.

To form the owl's body, bend the wire into a U shape, with 2 inches on each side and a 1-inch base. Apply glue along the base of the wire and jam it between the scales of the larger cone, 1 to 1½ inches from the cone's wide end. The ends of the wire should point upward.

Step 2.

Apply a drop of glue to each wire point. Lay the smaller pine cone on top of the larger, jamming the smaller pine cone onto the wire ends. The wide ends of the two cones should line up. Allow the glue to dry.

Step 3.
Glue eyes to upper part of smaller cone.

Step 4.
Cut "ears" from construction paper. Fold ears in half and glue to each side of the owl's head. Cut the beak from construction paper. Roll into a cone, and glue the wide end to the center of owl's face.

Step 5.
Place the owl on a forked tree branch.

24. Pine Cone Kitty

This cute kitty is fashioned from a slender pine cone with a tail made from a short, twisted piece of pod, a foxtail or similar brushy weed, shredded corn husk, or a piece of pipe cleaner.

Materials

Slender pine cone about 3 inches long and 1 inch in diameter

Heavy brown pipe cleaner

Thin pod, foxtail grass, shredded corn husk, or pipe cleaner

Scissors

Glue

Construction paper (red, black, or orange)

Several thin twigs

Step 1.

Cut a 4-inch piece of heavy pipe cleaner in half. Bend each section of pipe cleaner in the center, and jam the bend between the scales on the under- side of the cone to form pairs of legs, one near the front and one near the back. Adjust the pipe cleaners so that the cone will stand. Remove the pipe cleaners and apply glue at the bends, then glue to the underside of the cone.

Step 2.

Glue the tail to the top of the pointed end of cone.

Step 3.

Cut out 2 ears, 2 eyes, 2 pupils, and a nose from construction paper. Glue these features onto the flat end of cone.

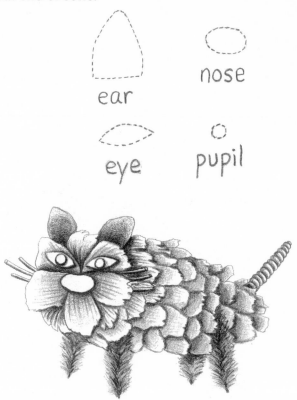

ear

nose

eye

pupil

Step 4.

Glue a few thin twigs on either side of the face for whiskers.

25. Pine Cone and Seedpod Chick

Create tiny chicks from small pine cones and sweet gum pods. You will need one cone and one pod for each chick.

Materials

    Small pine cone, about 2 inches long
    Sweet gum pod
    Feathers
    Medium-gauge wire, 4 inches long
    2 or 3 small feathers
    Contact cement
    Construction paper (yellow, brown, or orange)
    Small pliers
    Wire cutter

Step 1.
Glue the feathers to the top of the wide end of the pine cone.

Step 2.
Cut 1 inch off the wire and put aside. Bend the remaining wire into a U shape.

Step 3.
Apply a dab of glue to the rounded section of the wire and jam it between the scales on the lower end of the cone. Bend the ends of the wire forward to look like feet. Adjust so that the cone will stand.

Step 4.
Apply a dab of glue to one end of the 1-inch piece of wire and jam it into one of the holes in the sweet gum pod. Allow the glue to dry. Then apply glue to the other end of the wire and jam it into the top of the pine cone.

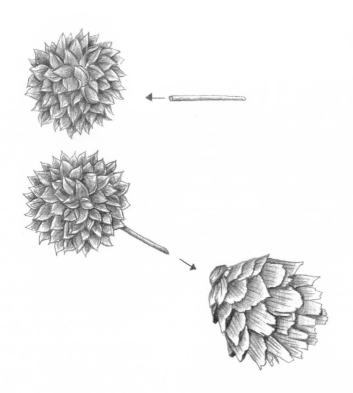

Step 5.
Cut the beak from construction paper. Fold it across the center and apply glue along the fold. Glue to the front of the sweet gum pod.

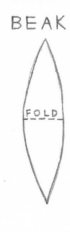

BEAK

FOLD

26. Teasel Insect

A teasel is a thistlelike plant with a spiny flower head. Teasels can easily be made into fanciful insects using scraps of wire, pipe cleaners, and imagination. Purchase plastic eyes in a craft or fabric store.

Materials

    Teasel flower head about 3 inches long
    Plastic eyes
    Thick pipe cleaner
    Thin-gauge brass or steel wire, 14 inches long
    White glue
    Needle-nose pliers
    Scissors
    Pencil
    Construction paper (optional)

Step 1.

Glue the eyes to the flat end of the teasel. Cut a small circle of construction paper for the nose and glue it in place, if desired.

Step 2.

Cut a 4-inch piece of pipe cleaner in half and bend each section into a U shape. Apply a dab of glue to the bend of each section, and jam the pieces into the spines on the underside of the teasel to form legs. One should be toward the front and one toward the back. Adjust the pipe cleaners so that the teasel stands.

Step 3.

Use the pliers to form wings by bending the wire into two loops. Twist the ends in the middle. Jam the center twisted section into the top of the teasel about one-third back from the face and secure with glue.

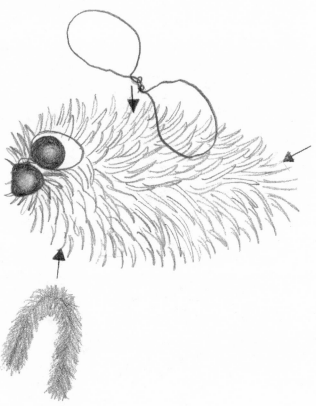

Leaves and Vines

We hail the merry autumn days,
When leaves are turning red;
Because they're far more beautiful
Than anyone has said.

—Charles Dickens

We are indebted to trees, shrubs, and bushes, for without them human life would not be possible. When leaves are exposed to light, they produce the oxygen we need to breathe.

Leaves come in many shapes and sizes. Although most leaves are green, they have many variations. Look at the landscape and count how many shades of green you see. In the fall, many leaves turn red, yellow, orange, and brown and drop to the ground. Other leaves remain green throughout the year. The underside of a leaf reveals a network of veins that bring nourishment to the plant.

A vine is a plant that trails along the ground unless it has a support to climb. Ivy is one type of vine. Its leaves remain on the plant all year long. Ivy is often trained into unusual shapes to create topiary.

27. Leaf Panels

When placed in a window, these leaf panels look almost like stained glass windows. For this craft, you will need to gather an assortment of leaves in various shapes and sizes. Although dry, brightly colored autumn leaves work best, you can also use fresh green leaves.

You will also use small scraps of crayons; you can recycle old, broken crayons that you might otherwise throw away. The leaves and crayon fragments are ironed between sheets of waxed paper. (Young children will require supervision.)

Place the finished panels in a window, where the light can pass through them to enhance the leaf forms and brilliant hues.

Materials
    Assorted leaves
    Waxed paper
    2 sheets of dark construction paper
    Old newspaper
    Scissors
    Ruler

Pencil
Broken crayons
Hand-held pencil sharpener or small knife
Iron
Ironing board or flat surface
White glue

Step 1.
Set up the ironing board and heat the iron to a medium temperature setting.

Step 2.
Place several layers of newspaper on the ironing board to protect the surface.

Step 3.
Cut four 5-by-8-inch pieces of waxed paper.

Step 4.
Place one piece of waxed paper on top of the newspaper. Arrange leaves on the waxed paper.

Step 5.
Remove the paper from the crayons and use a hand-held pencil sharpener or a small knife to cut shavings. Let the crayon fragments fall over the leaves. Keep the colors separate so that they will not run together when you iron them.

Step 6.
Place a second piece of waxed paper on top of the leaves and crayons and align it with the first piece of waxed paper.

Step 7.
Place two or three layers of newspaper on top of the waxed paper and leaves.

Step 8.
Carefully press with a hot iron. Lift up the newspaper to see whether the crayon has melted. Repeat if necessary.

Step 9.
Repeat the process with the other two pieces of waxed paper.

Step 10.
To make a frame for your panels, measure two 3½-by-6-inch "windows" in one piece of construction paper. Cut out the windows. Repeat with the second sheet of paper. The two pieces of construction paper must be cut identically.

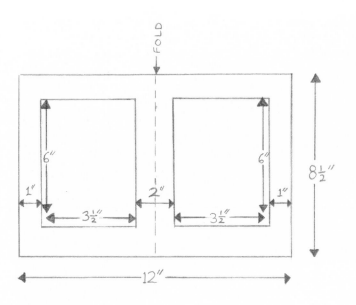

Step 12.
Place the second piece of construction paper on top of the first, being sure to align the windows. Glue the two pieces together to make a frame around the collages. Fold the construction paper in the center so that it will stand up to display the panels. Place the panels in a window.

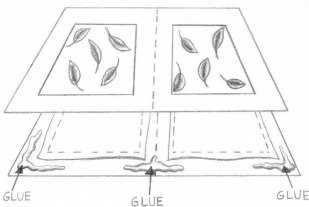

Step 11.
Lay one piece of cut construction paper on the work surface. Place the two waxed-paper leaf collages over the windows and glue in place.

28. Leaf or Pod Print Fold-Over Notes

Small leaves, fern fronds, or seedpods can be used to decorate these fold-over notes, which do not need an envelope. The design decorates the borders. The back of the note may also be decorated, but leave the front of the notes blank so that the address may be written. To mail the notes, fold them in three sections and seal with round self-adhesive stickers.

Make a set for yourself and another for a friend.

Materials
    8½-by-11-inch construction or art paper
    Tempera or acrylic paint, or water-based printing ink
    Small, flat leaves (such as ivy) or fern fronds, or seedpods with a flat surface (such as eucalyptus pods)
    Small paper plate
    Ruler
    Scissors
    Small, stiff paintbrush, ½ to 1 inch wide
    Self-adhesive stickers

Step 1.
For each fold-over note, measure and cut a piece of construction or art paper to 6 by 11 inches.

Step 2.
Pour a small amount of tempera or acrylic paint or printing ink onto a paper plate. A small amount of paint will print several cards.

Step 3.
Spread the paint evenly with brush.

Step 4.
Dip a small leaf, vein side down, in the paint. Make a sample print on newsprint or scrap paper to see whether you have too much or too little paint.

Once you've determined how much paint to use, dip the leaf again. Create a border design along the top edge of the notepaper by alternately dipping the leaf and pressing it onto the paper.

Step 5.
After the notes have dried, fold them in three sections. Make the first fold 3 inches from the top. This will serve as a flap to seal the note. The second fold should be made 7 inches from the top to create two equal sections of 4 inches each. (See pattern on next page.) Fold the lower section up to the first fold line.

Fold the 3-inch flap down. After you have written your letter, seal the flap in place with a sticker.

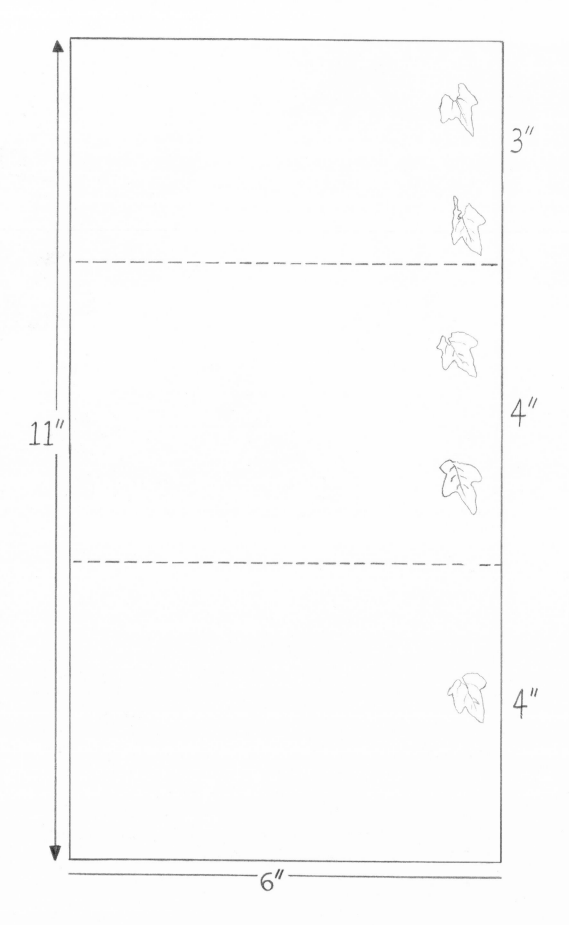

3"

4"

4"

11"

6"

29. Leaf Outline Greeting Cards

A handmade greeting card makes a thoughtful remembrance at birthdays and anniversaries. The elegant simplicity of leaf shapes makes them especially suitable for this project. For the most effective cards, select plain paper in a fairly deep color and a contrasting color of paint. Metallic print colors—gold, silver, copper—produce beautiful cards. You can use the pattern in step 7 to make an envelope for your card.

Materials

Construction paper
Bond typing paper
Leaves
Spray paint or tempera paint in a color that contrasts with the construction paper
Old toothbrush and stick (for tempera paint)
Old newspapers
White glue
Scissors
Ruler
Straight pins

Step 1.

Protect your work area with old newspapers.

Step 2.

Cut a piece of construction paper 9 by 6 inches. Fold it in half to make a 4½-by-6-inch card.

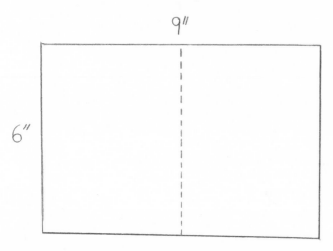

Step 3.

Place the card on the work surface with the fold to your left, opening to the right. Arrange one or more leaves on the front of the card and secure it with pins.

Step 4.

If you are using spray paint, shake the can, following the label's directions. Then spray lightly back and forth to paint the card. The areas covered by the leaves will remain unpainted. If you are using tempera paint, dip the toothbrush in the paint and shake off excess. Hold the toothbrush over

the paper, bristles pointing down. Move the stick back and forth across the bristles to create a fine spray of paint. Repeat until the area all around the leaves is speckled with paint.

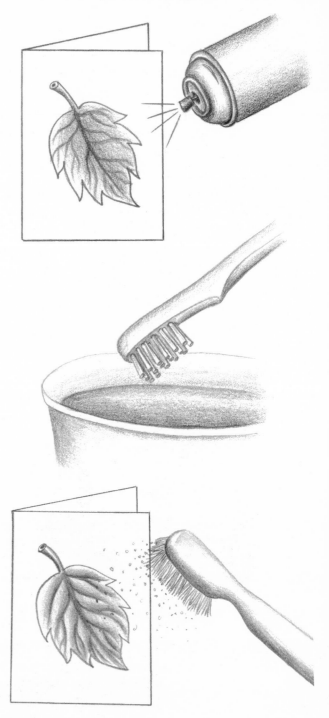

Step 5.

Allow the paint to dry, then remove and discard the leaves.

Step 6.

Cut a piece of bond paper 9 by 6 inches. Fold the paper in half to fit inside the card. Put a few drops of white glue along the inner fold of the card. Slip the insert inside the card with the folds aligned. Allow the glue to dry.

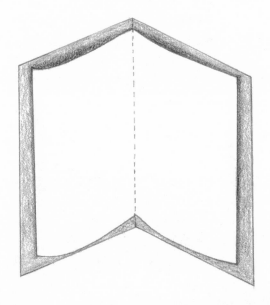

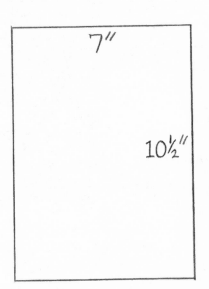

GLUE

Step 7.

Make an envelope for your card from bond paper, using the pattern below. If necessary, trim the edges of the card so that it will easily fit inside the envelope.

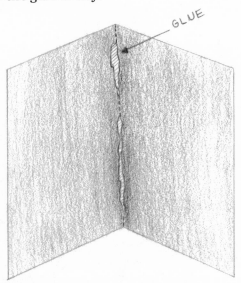

7″

10½″

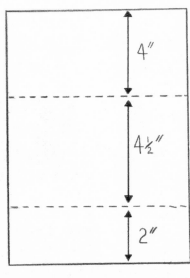

4″

4½″

2″

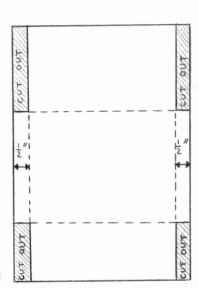

CUT OUT

CUT OUT

½″

½″

CUT OUT

CUT OUT

30. Leaf Tree Centerpiece

This miniature tree makes an attractive center-piece, especially for the holidays. You can quickly make this project using sprigs of leaves and a potato.

After the leaves wither, they can be replaced with fresh sprigs. Discard the potato when it begins to rot, but save your plaster-filled pot to use on another occasion.

Materials

Piece of cardboard
6-inch plastic or terra-cotta flowerpot
Coffee can or plastic container
½ cup water
1 cup plaster of paris
Stirring stick
10-inch dowel or straight stick
Potato
Sprigs of leaves from one kind of plant
Nail or other sharp tool
Colorful paper
Ribbon
Sphagnum moss

Step 1.

Cut the piece of cardboard to fit inside the bottom of the pot, and put it in place to cover up the drainage hole.

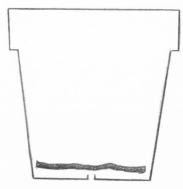

Step 2.
Pour ½ cup water into the can or container. Add 1 cup plaster of paris and stir until smooth. Pour the mixture into the pot.

Step 3.
After the plaster has set for about five minutes, poke the stick or dowel into the plaster, centering it in the pot. Position it so that it will stand straight. Allow the plaster to dry for at least an hour.

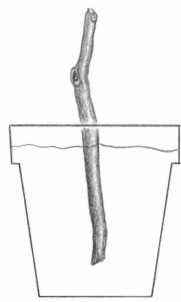

Step 4.
Using a nail or other sharp object, poke small holes in the potato. Press a sprig of leaves in each hole. Cover the entire surface of the potato in this fashion.

Step 5.
Press the potato onto the end of the stick or dowel to create a small tree. Cover the surface of the plaster with sphagnum moss and decorate the pot with colorful paper and a ribbon bow.

31. Ivy Topiary Wreath

Topiary is a Mediterranean art form in which vines, trees, or shrubs are trimmed or trained into unusual ornamental shapes. With a wire framework, vines can be used to create complex topiaries in various shapes, such as geometric figures or animals.

Making a simple ivy wreath is an easy introduction to the art of topiary. Decorated with a colorful red or green ribbon, this topiary wreath of small-leaf ivy makes a wonderful living holiday gift.

Materials

6 to 8 cuttings from small-leaf ivy (or 2 ivy plants)

Wire clothes hanger or medium-gauge wire, 36 inches long

Pliers

Flowerpot, at least 8 inches in diameter

Potting soil

Step 1.

Root the ivy cuttings in water or purchase two ivy plants. To root ivy, cut 1- to 2-foot lengths, pull off the bottom four or five leaves, and place the cut ends in a jar or glass of water. In about a week, roots will form, and the ivy is ready to pot. You may also plant two small ivy plants, but your topiary will take longer to grow.

Step 2.

Unbend the clothes hanger, using pliers. Shape the center part of the wire or clothes hanger into a circle or hoop, reserving 4 to 5 inches at each end.

Step 3.

Fill the flowerpot with potting soil. Moisten with water.

Step 4.

Press the ends of the wire hoop into the soil, and pat the soil to secure it. The base of the circle should touch the soil.

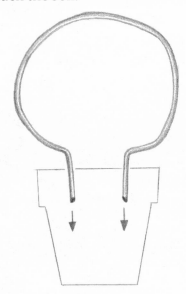

Step 5.

If you are using rooted cuttings of ivy, plant three or four on each side of the wire base. If you are using two small ivy plants, plant one on each side.

Press the roots of the ivy into the soil, making sure that they are covered.

Step 6.

Train or weave the ivy around the wire circle, being careful not to uproot the plants. If necessary, add a little more potting soil to protect the roots.

32. Leaf Fossil Medallions

Much of what we know about life on earth millions of years ago comes from fossils, the remains or imprints of plant and animal life preserved in rock.

Casting leaves in plaster of paris will leave a fossil-like impression. These small medallions may be hung in a window or worn on a cord as a necklace.

Materials

5 or 6 small leaves with interesting shapes and textures

Old newspapers

5 or 6 small paper cups (5- or 7-ounce size)

Coffee can or plastic container

½ cup water

1 cup plaster of paris

Stirring stick

Spray paint, gold paint, tempera paint, or acrylic paint

Paintbrush, ½ inch wide

5 or 6 medium nails

Yarn or cord, 4 inches long for a hanger, or desired length for a necklace

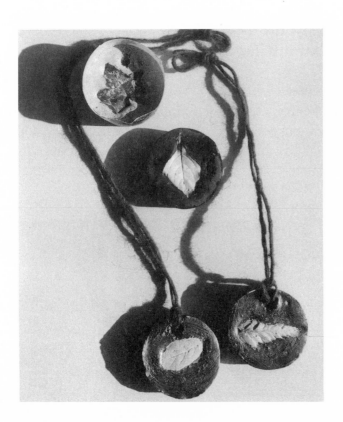

Step 1.
Gather an assortment of leaves small enough to fit flat in the bottom of the paper cups.

Step 2.
Cover the work space with old newspapers. Set out five or six paper cups.

Step 3.
Measure ½ cup water into the can or container. Add 1 cup plaster of paris. Stir the mixture until smooth. Add more plaster or more water to match the consistency of yogurt.

Step 4.
Pour approximately ½ to ¾ inch of plaster of paris into each paper cup. Allow the plaster to set for about five minutes.

Step 5.
Press a leaf into the plaster in each cup, with the vein side down. Gently rub the surface of each leaf to make an impression in the plaster. Do not remove the leaves.

Step 6.
With a nail, poke a small hole through each medallion. Leave the nails in place until the plaster dries. Gently jiggle the nails once or twice during the drying process so that they won't become permanently embedded in the plaster.

Step 7.
Allow the plaster to set for several hours until hardened. Once it has thoroughly hardened, tear away the paper cups and discard them. Remove the nails but do not disturb the leaves.

Step 8.
Paint the top surface of the medallions around the leaves. When the paint is dry, scrape away the leaves to reveal the impression of the leaves in the plaster. Thread a cord or piece of yarn through each hole to hang the medallions or to use for a necklace.

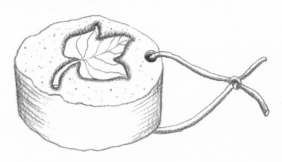

— 64 —

Flowers and Plants

*Summer breeze so softly blowing
In my garden pinks are growing;
If you'll go and send the showers
You may come and smell my flowers.*

—Old Garden Rhyme

Everyone loves the colors and fragrance of flowers. Although most flowers are associated with spring and summer, plants bloom at all times of the year. Flowers serve a useful function because they attract pollinating insects that help create seeds and thus enable the plant to reproduce itself. Other flowers are grown from bulbs. These bulbs reproduce themselves by creating more bulbs, which can be divided to make more plants.

Flowers can be appreciated in many ways. They can be picked and enjoyed fresh, pressed to retain their colors, or dried for bouquets that serve as reminders of the joys of spring and summer during the long winter months.

33. Summer Wreaths with Dried Flowers

Wreaths are symbols of hospitality that offer a charming welcome to visitors. They can also be used to decorate a patio or deck, and flower-trimmed garlands make lovely table centerpieces. Small wreaths and garlands are easy to make from bendable green twigs and vines. Dried foliage from daffodils and other bulb plants adds texture and strength. Decorate the wreaths with dried flowers and sprigs of weeds gathered on a walk. Finish with bows made of narrow ribbon. You can use the same technique to make larger or smaller wreaths, although larger wreaths are more easily made from vines. Start with a fairly small wreath to learn the technique.

Materials
    Bendable green twigs or vines
    Dried foliage from bulb plants or raffia
    Dried flowers and weeds
    Gardening gloves
    Clippers
    Scissors
    Narrow ribbon, ½ yard long

Step 1.

Gather green twigs or vines, such as ivy. Cut with clippers to lengths of at least 1 foot each. You will need at least four pieces to make a small wreath.

Step 2.

Strip off all leaves. You may need to wear gardening gloves to protect your hands.

Step 3.

Twist the twigs or vines together and shape them into a circle.

Step 4.

Using a long strand of raffia or bulb foliage, bind the twigs together by wrapping the strand over and under the bundle of twigs. If you are using dry foliage, first immerse it in water for five to ten minutes to make it more pliable. As you come to the end of the strand, tie it to the wreath and tuck the end between the twigs. Depending on the size of your wreath, you may need to use more than one strand.

Step 5.

Decorate the wreath by tucking dried flowers or decorative weeds among the twigs.

Step 6.

Tie a ribbon bow at the top or bottom of the wreath.

Step 7.

To hang the wreath, loop a piece of raffia around the top. Knot the ends and trim off the excess.

34. Victorian
Dried Flower Combs

Miniature rosebuds and small clusters of statice are just the right size to adorn these old-fashioned, romantic hair ornaments. Small rosebuds can be air-dried; statice is a naturally dry flower. You may also use petals, buds, or small blossoms from other dried flowers.

Make a pair for yourself and another for a friend.

Materials

2 plastic hair combs (3½ to 4 inches)

Narrow velvet ribbon, ¼ inch wide and ¼ yard long

Small rosebuds or the buds, petals, or small blossoms of other flowers

Clusters of statice

Heavy white glue or clear contact cement

Small scissors

Tweezers

Step 1.
Measure the velvet ribbon to cover the top of each comb. Cut the ribbon and glue it to the combs. Allow the glue to dry.

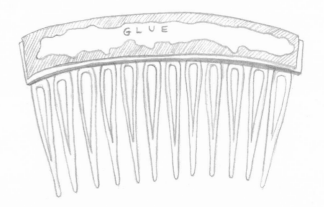

Step 2.
Trim away any stems from the miniature rosebuds or buds of other dried flowers. Pull small blossom clusters from a piece of statice.

Step 3.
Glue the flowers to the ribbon on each comb. Cluster the larger buds in the center of the comb, or space them evenly across the comb. Then use bits of statice to fill in the spaces between buds. Use tweezers to position tiny flowers. The flowers should not extend over the teeth of the comb. Allow the glue to dry thoroughly.

35. Candles with Pressed Flowers and Foliage

Candles decorated with pressed flowers, ferns, and leaves are delightful reminders of summer. You will need a chunky candle at least 3 inches in diameter. It can be round or square, short or tall. Purchase candles or make them yourself. The delicate hues of dried flowers show up best against white or pastels.

Materials
Candle at least 3 inches in diameter
Pressed flowers, leaves, and ferns
Waxed paper
Iron
Ironing board or other flat surface
Old newspapers

Step 1.

Place newspapers on the ironing board or flat surface to protect it from the melted wax.

Step 2.

Position the flowers, ferns, or leaves on one side of the candle and cover them with a piece of waxed paper.

flowers into the side of the candle. Wait five seconds before peeling off the waxed paper to see whether the flowers are secured in the candle wax. If necessary, repeat the process for five more seconds. Continue pressing flowers around the surface of the candle.

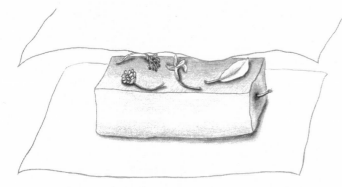

Step 3.

Heat the iron to a medium setting. Carefully press the iron over the waxed paper to embed the

Step 4.

While the candle is still warm, use your fingers to smooth the wax on the surface.

36. Pressing Flowers

Pressed flowers can be used in making stationery, greeting cards, place cards, wind chimes, and even a card game.

Pressing flowers is easy. You will need a large, thick book, such as an old telephone book; paper towels; and several weights, which might be bricks or additional books.

Gather small flowers from your garden or on a nature walk, carrying them home carefully so that they won't be bruised or crushed. Individual petals of large flowers may also be used, as well as colorful leaves.

Open the book. Place a piece of paper towel on the page for protection. Lay several flowers on the towel, using one kind of flower for each page. Do not let them touch one another. Place a second piece of paper towel over the flowers, and close the book carefully.

Materials

¼-inch plywood, 3½ by 7 inches
Ruler
Saw
Drill and bit
Sandpaper
4 1½-inch flat-head screws
4 wing nuts
Scrap corrugated cardboard
Bond paper

Repeat the process using other pages of the book. If you have a large number of flowers, you may need to use more than one book.

Place the book in a location where it will not be disturbed. Weight it down with several heavy books or bricks. Let the flowers dry for about two weeks.

You may also make a press from scrap wood, as detailed below.

Step 1.

Cut the plywood in half so that you have two 3½-by-3½-inch pieces. Sand the edges smooth.

Step 2.

Place one piece of the wood on top of the other. Measure ½ inch in from each corner and drill holes through both pieces of wood. The holes must be aligned through the two pieces of wood and must be large enough for the screws to pass through.

Step 3.

Cut nine pieces of cardboard and sixteen pieces of paper 3½ inches square. Cut all the corners off so that they will clear the screws when you stack them in the press.

Step 4.

Put the four screws through one piece of wood, from the bottom up; the screw heads are on the work surface. Place a piece of cardboard on the wood base. Next, put on a piece of paper. Arrange flowers and petals on the paper, and cover with a second piece of paper, then another piece of cardboard. Continue layering. Place the other piece of wood over the screws and use wing nuts to tighten the press. Allow the flowers to dry for several weeks.

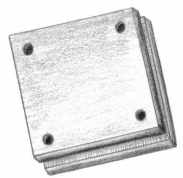

37. Pressed Flower Stationery

Make this stylish stationery by adorning plain white notepaper with a pressed flower or leaf. You can decorate the stationery with a single flower or a cluster of small flowers or with colorful autumn leaves. Use flowers or leaves you have pressed according to the directions in project 36. Each sheet of paper can have a different kind of flower or leaf.

A set of twelve sheets of stationery plus accompanying envelopes makes a thoughtful gift.

Step 3.
Center a blossom or a leaf at the top of one page of stationery.

Step 4.
Peel the backing from the piece of adhesive paper, and press the transparent film over the flower or leaf. Repeat for each piece of stationery.

Materials
   12 sheets bond paper, 6¼ by 8¾ inches (comes in a tablet)
   12 envelopes, 3⅝ by 6½ inches
   Clear adhesive paper, ½ yard
   Scissors
   Ruler
   Dried flowers and colorful leaves

Step 1.
Press an assortment of flowers or leaves, following the instructions in project 36. (Note: The flowers take two or more weeks to dry.)

Step 2.
Cut a square of adhesive paper slightly larger than the size of each flower, flower cluster, or leaf.

38. Flower Bookmark

Make these transparent bookmarks for yourself and for friends, using pressed flowers and leaves. If you don't want to wait several weeks for the flowers to dry, you may also use fresh flowers. They will keep their color for some time but will eventually fade. You can also add small feathers to your bookmark.

Materials

Assorted small flowers and leaves
Envelope
Clear adhesive paper, ½ yard
Scissors

Step 1.

Press an assortment of flowers and leaves, following the instructions in project 36. (Note: The flowers take two or more weeks to dry.)

Step 2.

Cut two 3-by-5-inch strips of clear adhesive paper.

Step 3.

Peel the backing from one strip of adhesive paper and place it sticky side up on your work surface.

Step 4.

Position the leaves and flowers on the sticky surface.

Step 5.
Peel the backing from the second strip of adhesive paper and place it sticky side down over the first sheet, being sure to align the edges. Smooth out any wrinkles.

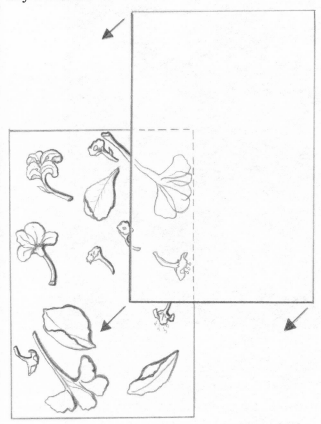

Step 6.
With scissors, round off the corners of the bookmark.

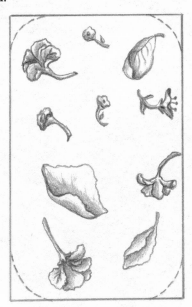

39. Rose Petal Beads

Making beads from rose petals is an old-fashioned craft that dates back hundreds of years. Rosaries used for devotion were often made from the fragrant petals of roses. Later, rose petal beads were sometimes made from the flowers in a bridal bouquet.

Roses are at their most fragrant early in the morning. Gather petals from roses in full bloom. If you don't have enough roses in your own garden, ask neighbors for permission to pick theirs. Use clippers to cut the blooms, then strip the petals into a paper bag. Watch out for thorns!

This recipe will produce enough rose petal beads for one necklace of fairly large beads.

Materials

  ⅔ cup flour
  3 tablespoons salt
  ⅓ cup water
  5 or 6 cups rose petals
  Food processor (optional)
  Large bowl
  Unflavored vegetable oil or rose oil
  Teaspoon
  Wooden toothpicks
  Cookie sheet
  Waxed paper
  Yarn, 2½ feet long
  Thread
  Needle with a large eye
  2 6-inch strips of narrow ribbon (for a
short necklace)

Step 1.

Measure flour, salt, and water into the bowl and stir with a spoon or mix with your hands until smooth.

Step 2.

Shred the rose petals into very small pieces. If you have a food processor, chop the petals finely. Add the rose petals to the dough and mix in with your hands.

Step 3.

Oil your hands with unflavored cooking oil or rose oil. Scoop the dough by teaspoonfuls and roll it into round balls. Try to make the balls approximately the same size. Push a toothpick through the middle of each ball to make a hole for stringing the beads.

Step 4.

Place the beads with their toothpicks on a cookie sheet lined with waxed paper and put it in the sun to dry. Turn the beads occasionally, reshaping if necessary so that they remain round. Depending on the weather, it will take several days for the beads to thoroughly dry. Bring the cookie sheet inside at night.

Step 5.

When the beads are dry, remove the toothpicks.

Step 6.

Cut the yarn to the desired length of the finished necklace plus 10 extra inches. Thread it into a needle with a large eye and string the beads. Knot the ends of the yarn several times to secure, and clip off excess yarn. You may also make a shorter necklace. Sew ribbons to each end of the yarn and tie the necklace in a bow at the back.

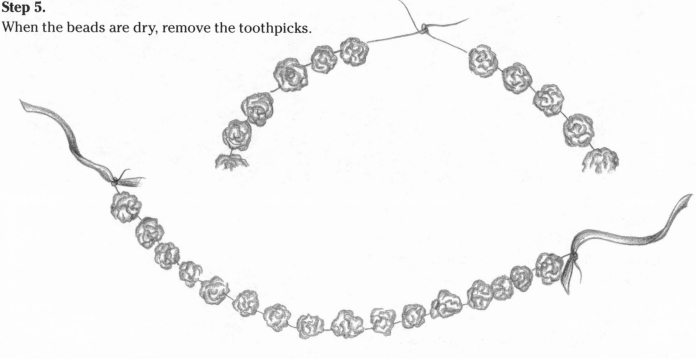

40. Flower Match Game

This variation of an old-fashioned game helps players develop memory skills while learning to identify wildflowers and leaves. The game is inexpensive to make, and because it is small, you can take it along to break the monotony of long trips. One to four people can play.

Materials

36 3-by-5-inch colored, unlined index cards

Clear adhesive paper, ½ yard

Two flowers or leaves from each of 18 kinds of wildflowers or trees

Pen

Field guides to wildflowers or trees

Step 1.
Collect pairs of 18 kinds of small flowers or leaves. Press, following the instructions in project 36. (Note: Items take two or more weeks to dry.)

Step 2.
Place each dried item in the top half of a card.

Step 3.
Cut a square of clear adhesive paper to cover each flower or leaf. Peel off the backing and position the transparent film over the flower or leaf. Continue until you have 18 pairs of cards.

Step 4.
Look up the names of the flowers or leaves you have selected. You can use the common or the botanical names, or both. Write the name of the flower or leaf in the lower half of each card.

To Play the Game
Mix the cards and spread all 36 on a table, face down. The cards should not overlap. The first player selects two cards and turns them face up.

If the flowers are the same, the player keeps the cards and draws two more, hoping to make another match. If the cards are not the same, the player returns them to the table, face down, in their original places. The next player takes a turn. The object of the game is to remember where each card is in order to pair them up. Participants learn the names of the leaves and flowers as they play.

Once all the cards have been paired, each player counts the number of cards he or she has. The winner is the player who has the most pairs.

This game also can be played by one person to improve the memory. Play as above, matching up cards until all are paired. You can set a time limit to see how quickly you can pair up all the cards.

41. Succulent and Cactus Terrarium

Terrariums are small gardens planted inside containers, such as jars and bottles. Cacti and other succulents, desert plants of the Southwest, can be grown in terrariums. You can start succulents by taking small cuttings from mature plants. Stick the end of the cutting in the soil, give it water and light, and the cutting will root.

Although terrariums are often made in elegant glass containers, you may also recycle a glass jar. Cover the print on the lid with a mosaic made of small dried beans or pebbles. Charcoal (which helps keep the terrarium fresh), perlite, vermiculite, and potting soil are available at a nursery or garden shop. Gravel, sand, and pebbles used in aquariums also may be added to the terrarium.

You do not need to water a desert terrarium very often. When the ground looks very dry, water gently. Use a spray bottle filled with water to mist the terrarium. Remove the lid from time to time if the inside of the jar gets too moist. When the plants outgrow the jar, transplant them to a flowerpot and replant the terrarium with small cuttings from the original plants.

Materials
    Glass jar with lid
    Charcoal (the kind used for potting plants)
    Potting soil
    Perlite, vermiculite, or small pebbles
    Small cacti or cuttings from succulents
    Long-handled spoon
    Chopstick or pencil
    Paper towel
    Dried beans or pebbles
    White glue

Step 1.
Wash and dry the jar, removing the label.

Step 2.
Place 1 inch of charcoal on the bottom of the jar.

Step 3.
Add 2 inches of potting soil over the charcoal. Pat down with a spoon.

Step 4.
Make small holes in the soil with the chopstick or pencil. Plant a small cutting or cactus in each hole. Use the tip of the pencil or chopstick to press soil around the cutting to secure it.

Step 5.
Moisten the soil with water. Do not make it soggy.

Step 6.
With the back of the spoon, make several indentations on the surface of the soil. Place a teaspoon of perlite, vermiculite, or small pebbles in each indentation to give texture to the terrarium.

Step 7.
With a paper towel, wipe the inside of the jar to remove any particles of dirt.

Step 8.
Decorate the jar lid with a glued-on mosaic of dried beans or pebbles (see project 3). Screw the lid onto the jar.

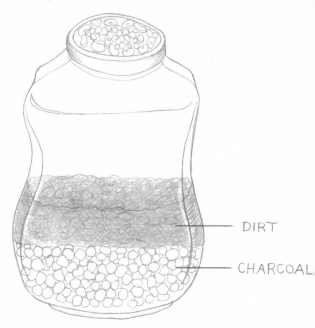

DIRT

CHARCOAL

42. Drying Flowers

Dried flowers and herbs make charming bouquets that continue to delight when summer is long past. Early settlers often gathered summer flowers to dry for winter bouquets.

Some flowers are naturals for dried arrangements. These include everlasting flower, sea lavender, statice, and yarrow. Seedpods and wild grasses also dry naturally and may be added to bouquets.

Other flowers must be dried by various methods. Herbs, hydrangea, and miniature roses may be air-dried. Tie the herbs in bunches and

hang them upside down; place hydrangea blossoms and roses in an empty vase. Let dry for two weeks.

Larger single blooms are best dried in a drying medium, such as silica gel, clean sand and borax, cornmeal and borax, or even cat box litter. The drying medium preserves the color and shape of the flower. Silica gel, which can be purchased in craft stores, probably produces the best results. Although it is the most expensive, it can be used over and over. Its primary advantage is that it does not damage the delicate petals.

Flowers do not dry at the same rate. Pansies and other small flowers dry quickly. Larger flowers, such as zinnias and large roses, take up to two weeks to dry.

Do not leave blossoms in the medium too long, or the petals will become brittle. The weather also plays a part—flowers dry more slowly in humid or rainy weather.

Materials

Drying medium: silica gel; one part borax plus two parts sand; one part borax plus five parts cornmeal; or cat box litter

Shallow box or cookie tin

Flower blossoms, such as zinnias, marigolds, pansies

Small, soft-bristle brush

Florist's tape

Florist's wire

Scissors

Attractive container

Step 1.
Pick perfect blossoms. Cut the stems to 1 inch.

Step 2.
Cover the bottom of a box or cookie tin with ½ inch of the drying medium.

Step 3.

Place the flowers face down on the medium. The flowers should not touch one another. Gently pour more of the medium around the flowers until they are completely covered. Do not cover the box, so that the moisture in the flowers can evaporate.

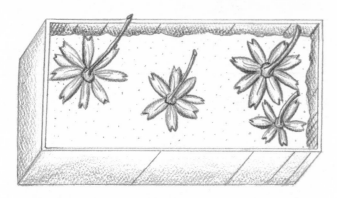

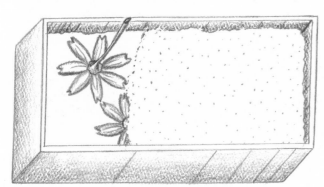

Step 4.

Allow the flowers to dry for four days to two weeks. Check them every few days until they are thoroughly dry.

Step 5.

Gently lift the dried flowers the medium. Use the small brush to dust off any of the medium that clings to the petals.

Step 6.

Mount the flowers on florist's wire as follows: Cut florist's wire to the length you need for an arrangement. Push one end of the wire through the base of each flower, and twist the wire around the inch of stem. Wrap florist's tape around the base and wire, continuing down the length of the wire stem.

Step 7.

Arrange the flowers in an attractive vase or other container.

43. Weed Pot Holder

Small dried weeds you find on your nature walks can make an enchanting arrangement for your home, especially attractive when they are displayed in this plaster of paris holder. The weed holder can decorate a porch or patio. If you use it inside, glue a small piece of felt to the bottom to protect tabletops.

Materials

Box or 5-gallon pail ½ full of moist sand
1 cup plaster of paris
½ cup water
Coffee can or plastic container
Stirring stick
Small, colorful pebbles and stones
7 or 8 medium-sized nails

Step 1.
Use your hands to make a 4-by-6-inch oval cavity that is ¾ inch deep. Smooth the sand.

Step 2.
Pour ½ cup water into the can or container. Add 1 cup plaster of paris and stir until smooth. Add additional water or plaster, if necessary, to match the consistency of yogurt.

Step 3.
Pour the plaster into the cavity in the sand.

Step 4.
As the plaster begins to harden, press small stones into the surface.

Step 5.

Poke seven or eight holes into the plaster with the nails, leaving them in the plaster. As it hardens, jiggle them a little so that they won't get stuck in the plaster.

Step 6.

Allow the plaster to dry and cure for about two hours before you lift the weed pot from the sand. Brush off excess sand and remove the nails. Stick a sprig of weed in each hole.

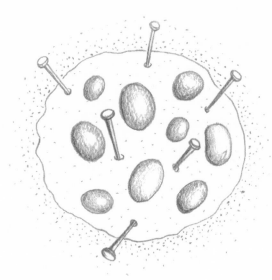

44. Floating Glow Candle

Flowers, water, and stones combine to make this unusual candle for a summer's eve. Simple flowers, such as daisies, are most effective. In the fall, use brightly colored leaves. To keep the flowers or leaves from floating to the surface, anchor them in pebbles or seashells collected at the beach or purchased at a garden aquarium store. Marbles can also be used.

You will need a clear glass container, such as a vase or glass. Add stones, flowers, and water, and float a walnut shell candle on the surface to illuminate the flowers. Flowers submerged in water last longer than they do in open air. Change the water when it becomes cloudy.

Materials

    Tall, clear glass container
    Clean pebbles, rocks, shells, or marbles
    Small flowers or leaves
    Water
    Walnut shell candles (project 20)
    Pebbles

Step 1.

Place a layer of pebbles, rocks, shells, or marbles on the bottom of the container as anchoring material. If you use stones or shells from the beach, wash them first in soapy water mixed with a teaspoon of ammonia, rinse well, and dry.

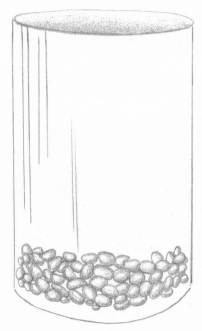

Step 2.
Cut the stems of the flowers or leaves so that the tops will be submerged when the container is filled with water.

Step 3.
Anchor the stems of the flowers or leaves in the pebbles or shells.

Step 4.
Add water to cover the flowers.

Step 5.
Float one or two walnut shell candles on the water and light them. Do not leave the candles unattended.

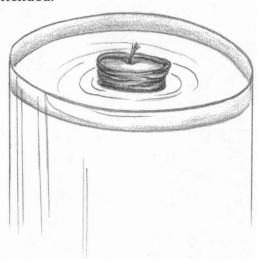

45. Transparent Pressed Flower Pictures

Pressed flower pictures were popular in the Victorian era. A transparent picture allows the light to pick up the delicate colors of the flowers and leaves. Make several pictures using flowers and colorful leaves of spring, summer, and fall. Hang the pictures in a window where the light can pass through them.

Materials
2 pieces of 5-by-6-inch clear glass
Glass cleaner and cloth or paper towel
Pressed flowers (project 36)
Clear cement glue
Fishing line or nylon filament
¾-inch colored mending tape
Scissors

Step 1.

Clean the pieces of glass. Lay one piece flat on your work surface. Arrange the pressed flowers in an attractive pattern on the glass.

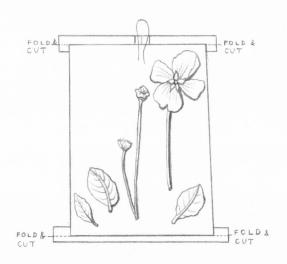

Step 2.

Cut approximately 2 inches of fishing line or nylon filament and form a loop. Glue the ends of the loop at the top of the glass.

Step 3.

Apply glue along the edges of the glass. Carefully position the second piece of glass over the first. Allow the glue to dry.

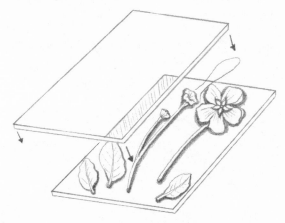

Step 5.

Press two 2½-inch-long pieces of tape to the top of the picture, one on each side of the fishing line, with the center of the tape at the top of the glass. Trim away excess tape.

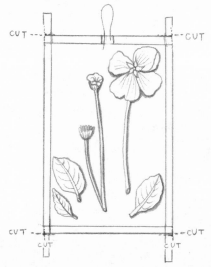

Step 6.

Apply tape along the sides of the picture to secure the glass; center the tape along the sides of the glass. Trim away excess tape.

Step 4.

Cut a 5-inch length of tape and pace it on your work surface, sticky side up. Stand the bottom edge of the glass picture on the center of the tape, lengthwise. Turn up the edges of the tape and press to the glass.

Eggs

Berryman and Baxter
Prettiboy and Penn,
And Old Farmer Middleton
Are five big men.
All of them are wanting
An egg for their tea,
But the Little Black Hen is much too busy,
The Little Black Hen is much too busy,
The Little Black Hen is MUCH too busy...
She's laying my egg for me!

—A. A. Milne

Eggs are one of nature's wonders. They are perfectly shaped, and they hold the potential of 61new life.

Eggs and eggshells can be used to make crafts. You can decorate them on the outside, you can crush them for mosaics, and you can empty them and use them as containers.

The most common eggs are the chicken eggs you buy at the supermarket. There are, however, other eggs in different sizes and colors, which can sometimes be purchased at farmers' markets.

46. Blown Eggs

Eggshells are the basis for many interesting craft projects. So that the eggs will last, remove the yolk and white by making a small hole at the top and at the bottom of the egg and blowing out the contents. Use the yolks and whites in cooking. Crafts made from eggs that are blown can last for many years.

Materials

Eggs
Long pin or needle
Bowl

Step 1.
Bring the eggs to room temperature.

Step 2.
With a clean pin or needle, poke a small hole at each end of the egg. The hole at the wider end of the egg should be larger. Then, through the larger hole, pierce and break the egg yolk.

Step 3.
Holding the egg over a bowl, blow through the hole at the narrow end to push out the white and the yolk.

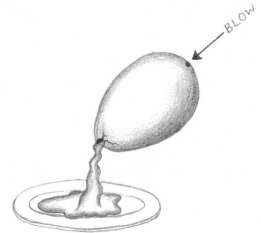

Step 4.
Rinse the eggshells with water inside and out. Blow the water out and let the shells dry. Store the blown eggs in an egg carton until you are ready to use them in a craft project.

47. Cut-Away Eggs

Decorating the inside of an egg is easier than it looks. An opening can be cut into the side of the egg using fine-pointed manicure scissors. Because the eggshell is very fragile, this process takes care and patience. The inside of the egg is then painted, and small dried flowers, such as miniature roses, are added, or tiny figures are used to create a scene. Decorative ribbon or braid glued on the outer surface of the egg provides additional strength. Egg ornaments make charming table decorations. To turn them into Christmas tree ornaments, use a needle to pull a length of thread through the decorative ribbon at the top of each egg.

Materials

Blown egg
White glue
Pencil
Pin
Manicure scissors with a fine point
Ribbon, lace, or braid
Gold spray paint or gilt paint
Watercolor brush
Paint thinner
Small dried flowers or tiny figures
¾- to 1-inch plastic drapery ring (available at fabric stores)

Step 1.

Draw an oval in pencil on one side of a blown egg. Make the oval a little wider at the wide end of the egg, which is the bottom of the ornament. Use the brush to apply glue around the outline to reinforce it. Allow the glue to dry.

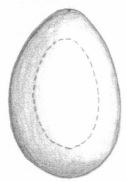

Step 2.

Poke a small hole in the center of the oval with the pin. Use manicure scissors to clip from this hole to the pencil line. Cut around the oval as evenly as possible.

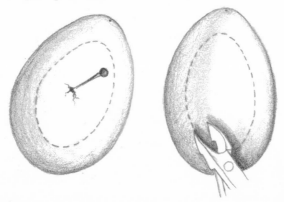

Step 3.

Paint the eggshell inside and out with gold paint and allow it to dry.

Step 4.

Cut a piece of ribbon, lace, or braid to fit around the opening. Dip the ends in glue to keep it from unraveling and allow them to dry. Fold the ribbon over the rough edge of the opening and glue it in place.

Step 5.

Glue additional strips of the ribbon, lace, or braid around the egg to decorate and reinforce the eggshell. The ends of the ribbon should meet at the narrow end of the egg.

Step 6.

If you plan to use your egg as a table decoration, glue a plastic drapery ring on the wide end of the egg to serve as a base.

Step 7.

Glue small dried flowers or miniature figures inside the egg. Glue a flower at the top where the ends of the ribbons meet.

48. Naturally Dyed Easter Eggs

Long before commercial dyes were available, people used berries, onion skins, nuts, and bark as tints. The custom of dyeing Easter eggs using natural materials was brought to America by German settlers. The eggs can be given a rich color by boiling them wrapped in onion skins secured with cheesecloth. The brown skins from yellow onions will dye eggs a rich yellow-orange; red onion skins produce a more delicate brown with a blue cast. Pressing leaves between the egg and the onion skins will make a soft design. Start by collecting enough onion skins to cover the surface of each egg. (Children must be supervised.)

Materials

    4 to 6 blown eggs
    White vinegar
    Onion skins, from yellow and red onions
    Small leaves or pieces of fern (optional)
    Cheesecloth
    Scissors
    Rubber bands
    Pan
    Slotted spoon
    Paper towels or napkins
    Glass canning jar or jar of similar size
    Spray lacquer or varnish

Step 1.
For each egg, cut a 4-inch square of cheesecloth.

Step 2.
Eggs have a natural protective film that resists

the dye. Wipe the eggs with vinegar to remove this coating.

Step 3.
Soak the onion skins. Wrap small leaves or fern fronds around the eggs (optional). Then gently wrap with damp onion skins. Keep the eggs wrapped with brown skins separate from those wrapped with red. Place each egg on a cheesecloth square. Gather the ends of the cheesecloth together and secure with a rubber band.

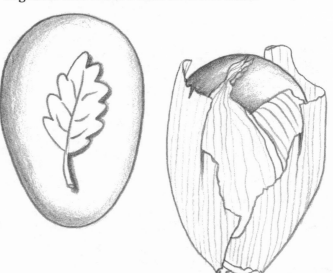

Step 4.
Place the eggs wrapped in brown skins in a pan of water. Bring the water to a boil. Float a glass jar on top of the eggs to keep them fully immersed. Reduce the heat and simmer for 15 to 30 minutes. The longer the eggs simmer, the deeper the color will be. Remove the pan from the stove and allow the water to cool before you remove the eggs.

Step 5.
Lift the eggs out of the pan with a slotted spoon. Rinse under cool water. Unwrap with care, as the eggs and onion skins may still be hot. Drain any water that might have gotten inside the eggs, blowing it out the holes if necessary. Blot the eggs with paper towels or napkins and allow to dry.

Step 6.
Repeat the process with fresh water for the eggs wrapped in red onion skins.

Step 7.
Spray the eggs with lacquer to provide a glossy finish and durability.

49. Moss-Covered Basket

Show off your naturally dyed eggs in this small moss-covered basket, which was made from a margarine tub. You may also display your eggs in a basket filled with natural grass (project 15).

Materials

Small plastic container, such as a margarine tub

Heavy-duty white glue

Pin or needle

Green floral wire, 12 inches long

4 or 5 bendable green twigs

Sphagnum moss

Step 1.
Wash the plastic container and dry it thoroughly.

Step 2.
With the pin or needle, poke two small holes on opposite sides of the container near the top for the handle.

Step 3.
Twist together four or five bendable green twigs to serve as a handle, and wrap with floral wire, leaving a few inches of wire at each end. Thread the ends of the wire through the two holes in the container from the outside in. Twist the ends of the wire up and around the handle to secure it.

Step 4.
With glue, cover a section of the outside of the plastic container and press into it a piece of the moss. Continue adding more glue and moss until the outside of the container is covered.

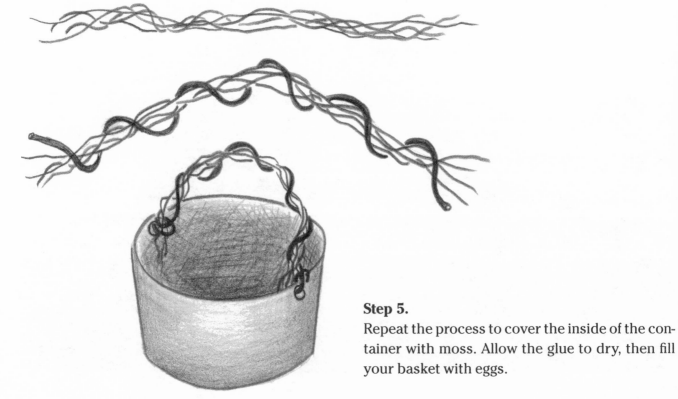

Step 5.
Repeat the process to cover the inside of the container with moss. Allow the glue to dry, then fill your basket with eggs.

50. Eggshell Mosaic

Eggshells can be crushed into small pieces, tinted with brilliant food colors or egg dyes, and used to create mosaics. The shell fragments produce a rich texture.

Make a cookie jar by gluing the fragments to the lid of an empty oatmeal box or coffee can and covering the container with decorative paper.

Materials
Eggshells
Food color, egg dyes, or fabric dyes
White glue
Pencil
Small brush
Small bowls
Paper towels
Teaspoons
Hot water
Decorative paper
Empty oatmeal box or coffee can
Salt or vinegar

Step 1.
Crush the eggshells into small fragments.

Step 2.
Pour small quantities of food color, egg dye, or fabric dye into small bowls. Choose basic colors— red, green, blue, yellow. Add several tablespoons of hot water to dilute each dye and a pinch of salt or a few drops of vinegar to fix the color. Place shell fragments in the bowls to dye them. When the shells reach the color you want, use teaspoons to lift them out of the bowls. Spread them out on paper towels to dry.

Step 3.
Cut a circle of paper to cover the lid of the container and glue it in place. Use a pencil to lightly draw your design. Simple shapes and designs are the most effective with these eggshell fragments.

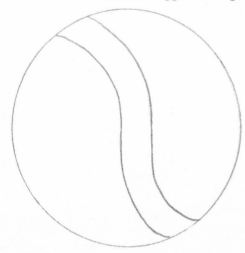

Step 4.
Paint one section of the design with glue.

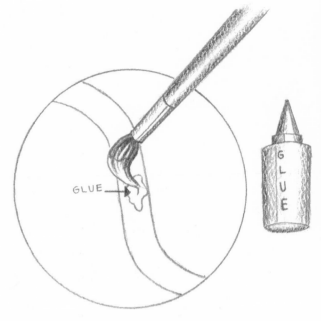

Step 5.
Cover that section with colored eggshell fragments. Shake off excess pieces. Paint a second section, and cover with another color of shell fragments. Repeat until you have finished your design.

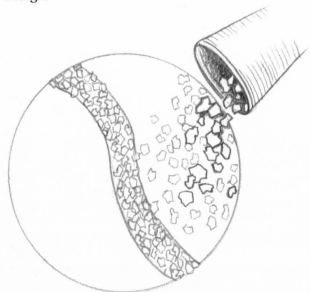

Step 6.
Cut a piece of decorative paper to cover the container and glue it in place.

51. Batik Eggs

Batik is an ancient process involving the use of wax and dye to create the designs on eggs and textiles. A design created with wax is protected from the dye, while the untreated area absorbs the color. Ukrainians, Russians, and other central Europeans are well known for creating intricately decorated eggs using a batik process.

Crayons and rubber cement can also be used as resistant materials to create designs on eggs. You can draw polka dots, stripes, or freehand designs on hard-boiled or blown eggs with a light-colored crayon, and use rubber cement to paint out larger areas that will resist the dye. After dyeing the eggs, you rub off the cement with your fingers, then use marking pens to draw designs in the blocked-off areas.

Dye hard-boiled eggs with food coloring or Easter egg dyes; do not use fabric dyes on eggs intended for food. If you plan to dye eggs as decorations, blow them out first.

Materials

    Blown or hard-boiled eggs
    Food color or egg dyes
    Vinegar
    Small bowl for each color
    Salt
    Water
    Teaspoon
    Paper towels
    Light-colored crayon
    Rubber cement
    Watercolor brush
    Marking pens

Step 1.

Eggshells are covered with a protective film; wipe them with vinegar to remove this coating so that they will absorb the dyes. Dry carefully.

Step 2.

Pour a small amount of food color into small bowls and add water to dilute the color. If you are using Easter egg dyes, dissolve the dye in a small amount of boiling water. Add a pinch of salt as a fixative. Allow the dye to cool to warm.

Step 3.

Use a light-colored crayon to draw stripes, dots, squiggles, or other designs on the eggs. Then, with rubber cement, block out larger areas, such as wide stripes, circles, or ovals. Use the brush that comes with the cement or a watercolor brush to make the designs. Allow the rubber cement to dry before you dye the eggs.

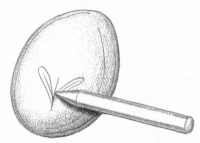

Step 4.

Place the egg in a dye. If you plan to dye the egg more than one color, place it in the lighter color first. A blown egg is hollow, so it will tend to float. Hold it down with a teaspoon so that it will dye evenly.

Step 5.

When the egg is colored, lift it from the bowl with the spoon, and pat it dry with a paper towel. If you wish to dye it a second color, use crayon or rubber cement to draw additional designs, then dip the egg in a darker hue.

Step 6.

If you are using blown eggs, blow air through the smaller hole to force out any dye that might be inside. Gently blot the eggs dry with paper towels.

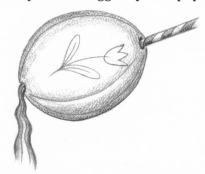

Step 7.

Remove the rubber cement by rubbing the eggs with your fingers.

Step 8.

Draw a design with marking pens in the areas that were blocked out with the rubber cement.

Twigs and Grasses

The oak is called the king of trees;
The aspen quivers in the breeze;
The poplar grows up straight and tall;
The pear tree spreads along the wall;
The sycamore gives pleasant shade;
The willow droops in watery glade;
The fir tree useful timber gives;
The beech amid the forest lives.

—Sara Coleridge

Trees are important to humans and animals alike. We use wood to construct houses and other buildings and to provide heat. Many birds and small animals also use trees to make their homes.

Sticks and twigs that you find on the ground can be used in various craft projects. You can also use the grasses and foliage that you find on your nature walks for weaving baskets and hangings.

The projects in this section all involve weaving. Weaving is an ancient craft in which some raw material, such as threads, yarn, rushes, grasses, twigs, or reeds are intertwined to create a fabric or basket. Perhaps humans learned to weave by observing birds and insects. Many birds weave nests to protect their young, and spiders weave webs that are works of art.

A woven fabric requires an interlacing of warp and weft. The warp consists of the threads that run lengthwise in the loom. The warp threads support the weaving. The weft, or woof, refers to the threads or fibers that cross the warp, interlocking with the warp threads to create a fabric.

A multitude of designs can be created by varying the way the weft crosses the warp. The crafts that follow use a simple over-and-under weave called a tapestry or tabby weave. In the first row of weaving, the weft fiber crosses over every other warp thread and under the others. In the second row, the weft fiber crosses in the reverse.

Tapestry weavings may be very simple or very complex. Intricate tapestries from the Middle Ages, which once decorated the walls of castles, may be seen in museums. Native American rugs and blankets are also a form of tapestry weaving.

52. Salt Box Treasure Basket

Some Native American basket makers wove baskets trimmed with feathers and beads as special gifts, often for wedding couples. Today these trimmed baskets are still greatly valued. To create a basket with a similar feeling, weave the basket over a cardboard salt container and decorate it with small feathers. Most salt boxes have a circumference of 11 inches. The width of the warp spokes can be wide or narrow, but you must have an uneven number.

Materials

Round cardboard salt container, empty
Scissors
Raffia or dried foliage from bulbs
White glue
Small feathers
Ruler
Pencil

Step 1.
Remove the paper label from the salt box. Cut the salt box in half horizontally. Use the half that does not have the metal pouring spout.

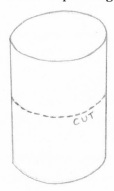

Step 2.
Make marks at 1-inch intervals around the circumference of the basket. Cut a vertical slit from each mark to the bottom of the cardboard but do not cut into the white paper that covers the bottom

of the box. Push the warp spokes outward to form a bowllike shape.

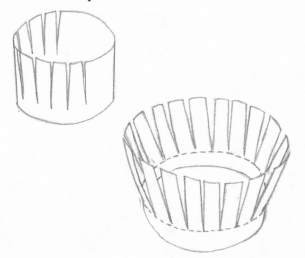

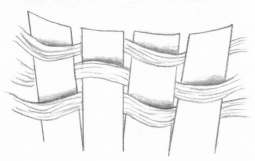

Step 4.
Spread glue on the white paper base of the salt box, and wrap additional fiber around the base to cover the white paper. Fasten the ends with a pin while the glue is drying. You may also cover the cardboard inside the bottom of the basket with fiber. Allow the glue to dry.

Step 3.
Starting at the base of the box, tuck a piece of raffia or bulb foliage under one warp spoke. Weave the fiber over and under, over and under the warp spokes, adding fiber when necessary. Tuck loose ends into the weft as you weave. Push the weft down tightly as you cover the cardboard spokes and secure the weaving. Weave to the top of the box. On the last row, wrap the fiber around each warp spoke. Put a drop or two of white glue at the top of each spoke to further secure the weft.

Step 5.
Tuck the tips of small feathers into the fiber around the outside rim of the basket.

53. Bird's Nest Basket

Birds make use of all types of natural materials to make a cozy nest for their young. You can create a similar basket using materials found in your backyard or a park.

Materials

10 bendable sticks or twigs, at least 12 inches long

Raffia or foliage from bulbs

Decorative dried flowers, weeds, and ornamental grasses

Step 1.

Take four twigs or sticks and arrange them in a crisscross fashion. Tie with raffia, fiber, or string to secure the twigs.

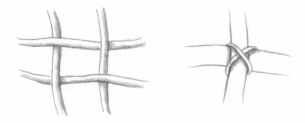

Step 2.

Take a piece of raffia or foliage and tie it to one of the crisscross sticks. Begin weaving from right to left as follows: Weave the fiber under the second cross, over the third cross, under the fourth, and back over the first. Twist the raffia around the first stick one time. Now weave the fiber over the second cross, under the third cross, and over the fourth cross to further secure the base of the basket.

Step 3.

Add an additional twig, weaving it into the crossed twigs at a diagonal from right to left. You now have five twigs, thus ten twig ends in the warp.

Step 4.

Gently pull all the twigs upward to form a bowl shape.

Step 5.

Weave the fiber over one twig and under the next. Continue over and under, over and under around the basket. When you reach the tenth warp twig end, wrap the fiber around it once or twice to alternate the weave. Vary the weft by changing back and forth from fiber to soft twigs every three or four rounds. Continue weaving until you reach the tips of the warp twigs.

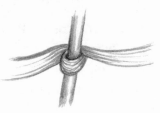

Step 6.

To secure the weft, finish the basket: Use fiber to weave the last two or three rows. On the last row, wrap the fiber around each warp twig end several times. Tuck all the loose ends into the warp.

Step 7.

To give your basket the appearance of a real bird's nest, tuck small bits of dried flowers, weeds, and ornamental grasses into empty spaces in the basket, securing them behind a warp twig.

54. Fiber Tapestry

Create this simple fiber tapestry or wall hanging to show off some of the treasures you have collected on nature walks.

The variety of materials that can be woven into a fiber tapestry is limited only by the imagination. Bits of fur you save from combing your dog or cat, feathers gathered on a walk, dried weeds and leaves, strips of bark, corn silk, and small lengths of cotton or wool yarn are just some of the materials that can be used to create an interesting sculptural tapestry.

This tapestry is woven on a loom made from a cardboard box or lid, and cotton string serves as a warp or framework for the weaving. The number of warp threads depends on the size of the lid, but it must be an odd number. The weaving in the photo has thirteen warp threads.

Hang the finished tapestry from a piece of driftwood you discovered at the beach or a twisted branch you found on the ground in the woods.

Materials

    Cardboard box or lid
    Scissors
    Medium-weight yarn, several yards
    Ball of cotton string
    Assorted feathers, fur, dried flowers,
grasses, weeds
    Driftwood or bare branch
    Small nails or push pins
    Hammer

Step 1.
Cut an uneven number of 1-inch slits in one edge of the box or lid. The slits should be ½ to 1 inch apart.

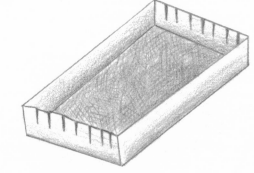

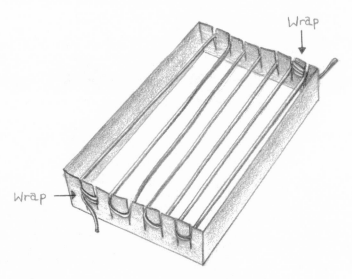

Step 2.
Cut the same number of slits in the opposite edge, spaced just the same.

Step 3.
To warp your loom, start at one bottom corner of the box. Pull a length of cotton string from the ball and wrap the end several times around slits 1 and 2 to secure it. End at the slit nearest the edge, slit 1.

Pull the string to the top and wrap it around the first two slits. Pull to the bottom and wrap it around slits 2 and 3.

Pull to the top, and wrap the warp around upper slits 2 and 3.

Keep the tension even. Continue warping the string up and down. Wrap the end around the last two slits several times to secure, and cut off the string.

Step 4.
Start the weft by weaving about 3 inches from the bottom of the loom. Cut a piece of yarn six or seven times the width of the loom. Starting at the right edge, weave over the first warp thread, under the second, over the third, and so forth, ending the row with an under weave at the left edge. Pull the yarn through the warp threads, leaving a 3- to 4-inch tail at the right side.

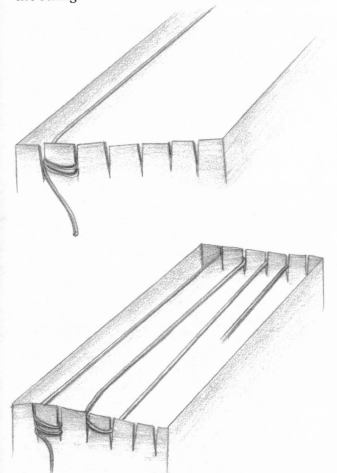

Step 5.
For the second row, start at the left edge and weave over the first warp, under the second. Continue to the end of the row. With your fingers, push the yarn of the second row down to touch the first row. Continue weaving back and forth until you have six or seven rows. The exact number is not important.

Step 6.
Weave a piece of bark or grass into the next row following the over-and-under, over-and-under pattern. For three or four rows, weave with found objects, such as fur, feathers, or corn silk.

Step 7.

Cut another long piece of yarn. Starting at the left side, weave five or six rows in the over and under, over and under pattern to secure the found objects. Then add three or four more rows of found objects. Continue weaving, alternating found objects and yarn, until you are approximately 5 inches from the top of the loom.

Step 9.

Hammer a row of six or seven nails or tacks into the driftwood or branch. You may also use tacks or push pins.

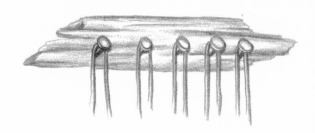

Step 10.

Push the bottom six or seven rows of weft up the warp threads so that they are close to one another. Cut the bottom of each loop of warp to make two threads. Tie pairs of warp threads in hard knots to secure the weaving. Weave any loose ends of yarn into the back of the tapestry. To hang the tapestry, hook each loop of warp at the top over a nail or tack in the driftwood or branch. Hang your tapestry on the wall or suspend it from a low branch in your yard.

Step 8.

Weave the last five or six rows with yarn. On the last row, tie a knot with yarn around each warp thread. Carefully lift the tapestry from the loom.

55. Branch Weaving

A forked branch makes a good loom for an interesting outdoor hanging. Look for a forked branch about 15 to 20 inches long and 12 to 15 inches wide at the tips of the arms.

Use rough twine to make a warp for the loom. The weft is made of treasures discovered on nature walks. Look for strips of bark, small twigs, grasses, weeds, feathers, and wildflowers to create the weft. Weeds and wildflowers are especially attractive against a bark background.

The weft can incorporate more than one material. After weaving a strip of bark, for example, work feathers or flowers into the same row, following the same under-and-over, under-and-over pattern of the bark. The second layer adds strength as well as texture and visual interest.

Materials

    Forked branch
    Saw, loppers, or heavy clippers
    Twine
    Leaves, feathers, bark, fur, dried wildflowers,
weeds, and grasses
    Large bead
    Scissors

Step 1.

Use a saw, loppers, or heavy clippers to cut off
the base of the forked branch, leaving a V shape.

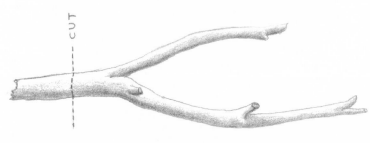

Step 2.

Cut a long strip of twine. To wrap the warp around
the branch, hold the branch so that the wide part
of the V is pointing toward the right. Securely tie
the twine near the end of the lower branch. Pull
the warp to the upper branch, keeping the tension
tight, and wrap it around the branch twice. Pull
the twine to the upper branch and wrap it around
twice. Space the warp threads at 1½- to 2½-inch
intervals. Pull back down to the lower branch
and wrap twice. Continue wrapping the warp in
this manner until you reach the base of the V.
You must have an odd number of warp threads.
Tie the last warp thread securely on the reverse
side of the branch so that it doesn't show.

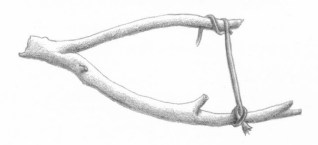

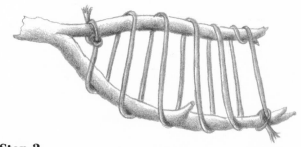

Step 3.

Weave from the bottom up. Starting at the lower
right corner, weave grasses, strips of bark, corn
husks, dried flowers, leaves, and weeds into the
warp. Weave under the first warp, over the second,
under the third, and so on. For the second row,
weave back from left to right in reverse fashion—
over, under, over, under. Continue weaving until
you have filled in most of the space between the
sticks.

Step 4.

Cut a piece of twine about 20 inches long. Tie one
end on the right end and the other on the left end
of the upper branch. Make a loop in the center of
the twine. Tie a knot about 3 inches from the top
of the loop. Thread a large bead so that it rests
on the loop, and tie a second knot on top of the
bead to keep it in place. To hang the weaving,
hook the loop over a nail.

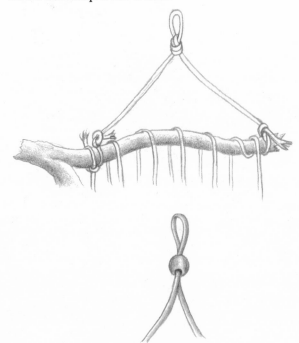

56. Eye of God

The eye of God, a decorated cross woven with yarn and natural fibers, is a popular folk art decoration in Mexico. Eyes of God can be very small or very large. They are often used in groups. In this version of the craft, small sticks or twigs are woven with natural grass fibers and yarn.

Materials

2 twigs, one 7 inches long, one 6 inches long
Raffia or dried bulb foliage
Yarn, medium weight

Step 1.

Holding the longer stick vertically and the shorter stick horizontally, place the shorter stick over the longer stick to form a cross.

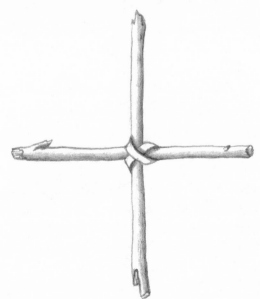

under, over and under each stick. Continue for about eight rounds, ending at the top. Tuck the end of the raffia into the weaving.

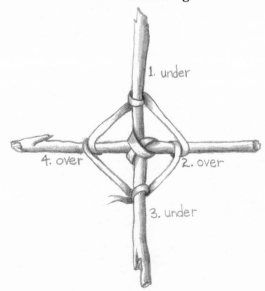

Step 2.

Tie the sticks together with a long piece of raffia or dried bulb foliage. Weave the raffia clockwise around the cross, wrapping the fiber over and

Step 3.

Tie a piece of yarn to the top stick. Continue weaving clockwise as above. Weave about eight rounds. Cut or break off the yarn, leaving a 1-inch end. Tie the end to the top stick to secure it, and tuck the end into the yarn weaving.

Step 4.

Tie another piece of raffia or bulb foliage to the top stick. Weave around each stick as above until you reach about 1 inch from ends of the sticks. Tie the raffia to one of the sticks to secure it, and tuck the end of the raffia into the weaving.

Step 5.

Tie another piece of yarn to one of the sticks and weave to about ½ inch from the top of the cross.

Tie the yarn to the top stick. Trim it, leaving a piece about 1 inch long. Weave the excess yarn into the weaving.

57. Dream Catcher

Dream catchers were sometimes made by Native American mothers, who suspended the dream catchers over their babies while they slept. It was believed that bad dreams were caught in the web, but good dreams were allowed to pass through. Dream catchers make interesting hanging ornaments for the patio or garden.

Materials
    Bendable green twigs
    Thin brass wire, 22-gauge or finer
    Thin leather thong, 6 inches long
    2 beads with holes to fit the thong
    4 feathers
    Fishing line or nylon filament
    Scissors
    White glue
    Ruler

Step 1.
Bend the twigs into a circle, twisting them around one another so that they will hold together. The circle should measure about 5 inches across and have a thickness of four to five twigs. Wrap a small piece of wire around the ends to secure the twigs.

Step 2.
With the scissors, cut about 20 inches of wire. Anchor the wire to the circle by twisting it around the edge several times. Weave back and forth across the circle to make a web, wrapping the wire twice around the twigs wherever it touches

the circle. You will go back and forth three or four times.

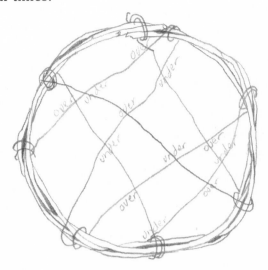

Step 3.

Cut another piece of wire about 20 inches long and continue weaving over and under the first wires until you have created a web of wire inside the circle.

Step 4.

Tie a 6-inch piece of leather thong at the bottom of the circle so that there are two equal lengths hanging down.

Step 5.

Thread each end of the thong through a bead. Put a drop of glue into the bead hole. Push two small feathers into the holes of the bead alongside the thong. Allow the glue to dry.

Step 6.

Tie a piece of fishing line at the top of the circle for a hanger. Suspend the dream catcher from a nail or a branch.

Fruits

A little peach in the orchard grew—
A little peach of emerald hue;
Warmed by the sun and wet by the dew,
It grew.

—Eugene Field

After flowers bloom and fade away, some plants and trees produce fruits that can be used in projects. Some of the projects included here use fruits in unusual ways, and others make tasty treats.

You can purchase the fruit for these projects at the grocery store or harvest them yourself. You may find some fruits growing wild, but you must know what you are picking, because some are poisonous. Whether you purchase your fruit or harvest it yourself, be sure to use the fruit fairly soon, as it can be quick to spoil.

58. Pomander Balls

Pomander balls, one of the oldest air fresheners, are made from citrus fruit and aromatic spices. Centuries ago, during the Renaissance, ladies carried pomander balls in beautifully designed balls of silver and gold to help cover the bad smells of the city.

Today, pomander balls made from citrus fruits studded with cloves can be used in linen drawers and closets to give a fresh, spicy scent to sheets, towels, and clothing. As the orange or lemon shrivels, the oils of the rind blend with the aroma of the spices. Pomander balls make welcome gifts.

Materials
Old newspaper
Small nail or corncob holder
Small orange or lemon
Whole cloves
Ribbon or yarn
Scissors
Paper or plastic bag
2 to 3 tablespoons powdered cinnamon or allspice

Step 1.
Cover your work surface with newspaper.

Step 2.
Using a small nail or corncob holder, pierce holes in the rind of the orange or lemon. Then press in cloves, covering the entire surface.

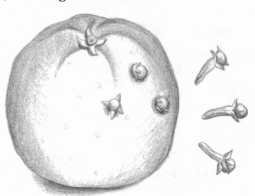

Step 3.
Measure a piece of ribbon to fit around the center of the fruit, adding 8 inches, and cut. Center the fruit on the ribbon, and tie it around the fruit from bottom to top. Tie a bow at the top.

Step 4.
Measure a second length of ribbon to fit around the fruit, adding 8 inches, and cut. Wrap this ribbon securely around the fruit from bottom to top, dividing the fruit into quarters. Tie a second bow at the top.

Step 5.
If you want to hang the pomander ball in a closet, tie a loop of ribbon to the bow.

59. Apple Head Doll

An apple head doll is a traditional American craft that recalls an earlier and simpler time. An apple is carved to form the doll's head. As the apple dries, it shrivels to resemble the wrinkled face of an elderly person. The body is easily constructed from wire and old nylon pantyhose. The pattern for the doll's costume is to scale for an 11- or 12-inch doll; the wire armature is shown half-scale.

Materials

Medium-sized Delicious, McIntosh, or Jonathan apple without blemishes

Paring knife

2 whole cloves

Lemon juice or a solution of half vinegar and half water

Wire coat hanger

2 pairs of old pantyhose

Calico cloth, ¼ yard

Pliers

Scissors

Watercolor, acrylic, or tempera paint

Step 1.

Peel the apple and remove the stem.

Step 2.

Carve the face. Hollow out the eye sockets about one-third down from the top of the apple, and carve the mouth about one-third up from the bottom of the apple. Carve a definite chin and a fairly wide nose, because the features will shrink as the apple dries.

Step 3.

Brush the apple with lemon juice or a solution made of half vinegar and half water to keep it from turning too dark. Insert a clove into each eye socket.

Step 4.

Poke a piece of wire through the apple from top to bottom and make a loop at each end. Hang the apple head to dry for three or four weeks. Check the apple every week to adjust and mold the features.

Step 5.

When the apple is ready, it will still be slightly soft to the touch. Remove the wire by untwisting the bottom loop. You may leave the cloves in the eye sockets or remove them. You may paint the face if you wish, and you may also lacquer the apple to make it more durable. Glue cotton or wool on the head for hair.

Step 6.

To create a body, unwind a wire coat hanger. Use the pliers to twist the wire into a body shape. The body size should be in proportion to the dried apple head. Cut the legs from two pairs of old pantyhose and wrap them around the wires to from a body. Tie securely and tuck in the ends.

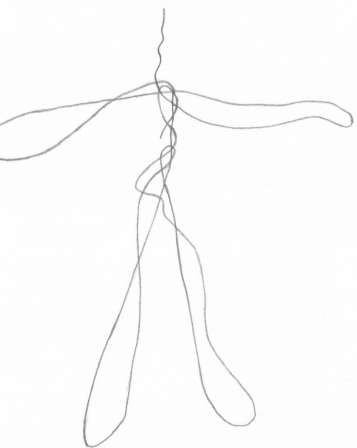

Step 7.

Cut out and sew a simple dress from calico. (See pattern next page.) You may add an apron, hat, scarf, or other details as desired.

Note: The pattern for the clothes is to scale for an 11- or 12-inch doll. The drawing for the wire armature is about half size. Some apples will shrink more than others.

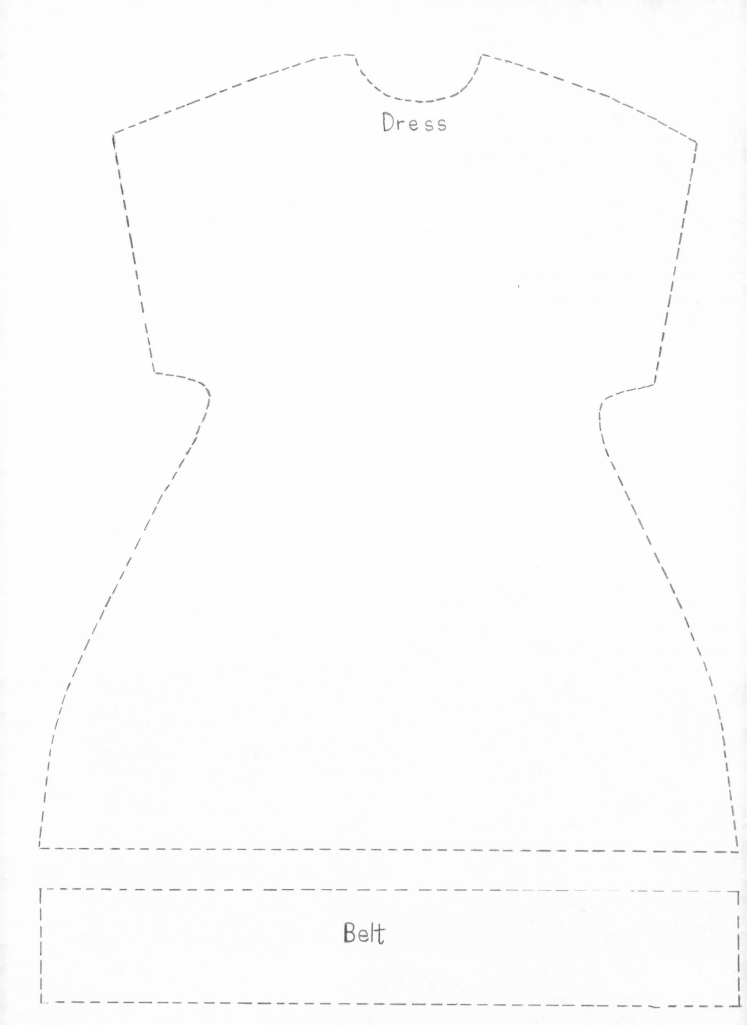

Dress

Belt

60. Fruity Fleet

Young children will enjoy making sailboats from orange, lemon, and lime rinds. Hollow out the rinds and add a mast and a construction paper sail. Keep your fruit boats in the refrigerator until you're ready to set sail in the bathtub or pond. These boats actually do float.

Materials
  Orange, lime, or lemon
  Serrated knife
  Scissors
  Clay or Play-Doh
  Twigs (3 inches long for oranges or large lemons, 2 inches long for limes)
  Construction paper
  Scissors
  White school glue or paste

Step 1.

Cut the fruit in half, either lengthwise or across the width. Using a serrated knife, scrape the pulp out of the fruit. Set aside for another use.

ORANGE

LIME

Step 2.

Place a small wad of clay or Play-Doh in the bottom of the fruit shell, and stick in the twig mast.

Step 3.

Cut out the sail from construction paper and fold it in half. Glue it around the mast. Allow the glue to dry before sailing time.

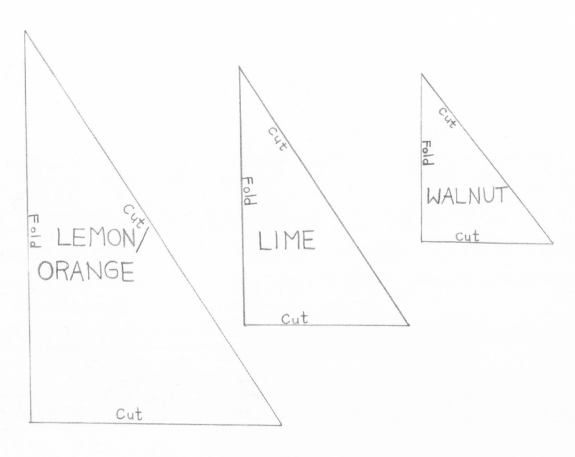

61. Fruit Leather

Fruit leather and fruit rolls are easy and inexpensive to make at home, especially during the summer when fruit is abundant. Fruit leather does not require elaborate equipment and thus is an easy project for children as well as adults. The results are nourishing, translucent snacks.

You can make fruit leather from almost any pulpy fruit, but citrus fruits and melons contain too much juice to dry well. In addition to berries, peaches, apricots, and plums, you may want to try more exotic tropical fruits like mangoes and papayas, which can be blended with peaches and nectarines to make unusual treats not available commercially. You can combine a variety of fruits for unusual flavors; use fruits of compatible colors. For a marbled effect, place two fruits side by side on the drying surface and swirl them together. Spices such as cinnamon, allspice, or nutmeg will add extra zip.

Fruit leather is dried naturally by sunlight or in the oven with very low heat. The pilot light of a gas oven will provide enough heat. An electric oven should be kept at the lowest possible temperature, around 125° F.

Store fruit leather by rolling it up in plastic wrap. Fruit leather will keep for about a month at room temperature and can be stored in the refrigerator for up to a year.

Materials

Cookie sheet
Pan
Large spoon
Plastic wrap
Blender
Screen or cheesecloth
Measuring cup and spoons
About 1 pound of fresh fruit, to make 2 cups chopped
3 tablespoons sugar (optional; you may use less)
1 tablespoon lemon juice (not needed for plums)

Step 1.

Wash, pit, peel, and chop the fruit to make approximately 2 cups. (Apricots and plums do not need to be peeled.)

Step 2.

Place the fruit in a pan. Add sugar and lemon juice. Cook the fruit over medium heat for about 5 minutes, mashing it with a spoon and stirring constantly to avoid scorching. Do not add any extra liquid. Remove the pan from the heat and allow the fruit to cool slightly.

Step 3.

Puree the mixture in a blender or beat it by hand. It is not necessary for the mixture to be completely smooth.

Step 4.

Line a cookie sheet with plastic film. Spread the fruit evenly to the edges of the plastic film. The thinner the fruit is spread, the faster it will dry.

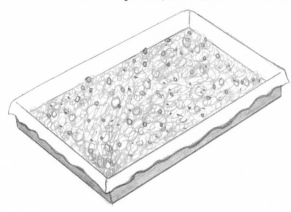

Step 5.

Put the cookie sheet in the oven, or cover it with a wire screen or cheesecloth to protect the fruit leather from insects and place it in the sun. If you've set it outdoors, check it from time to time to make sure that the fruit is not attracting insects. If the fruit is not dry by the end of the day, bring it inside for the night and return it to the sun the next day. Fruit leather is dry when it can be peeled off the plastic.

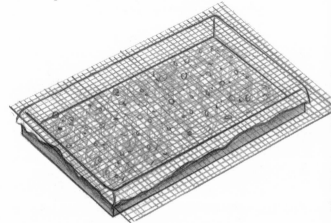

Here are some specific recipes. You may vary them by using other fruits.

Apricot Fruit Leather

1 pound apricots, or 2 cups halved
3 tablespoons sugar
2 tablespoons grated lemon or orange rind

Halve unpeeled apricots and remove the pits. Place in a heavy pan with sugar and citrus rind. Cook 5 minutes. Cool slightly. Puree the fruit and allow it to dry on plastic wrap.

Plum Fruit Leather

1 pound plums, or 2 cups chopped
3 tablespoons sugar

Pit the plums and measure 2 cups of pulp. Heat it to the boiling point. Add sugar. Puree the fruit. Spread it on plastic wrap to dry.

Tropical Fruit Leather

1 soft mango
1 or 2 peaches or nectarines
2 tablespoons sugar or honey
1 tablespoon lemon juice
½ cup shredded dry coconut

Peel the mango and remove the pulp from the seed. Peel and slice the peaches and add them to the mango pulp to make 2 cups. Place the mixture in a heavy pan with lemon juice and sugar or honey. Cook over medium heat until bubbly, mashing the fruit with a spoon. Cool. Puree the fruit. Add coconut. Spread out on plastic wrap to dry.

62. Potato Prints

Wood block prints have been popular in Japan for many centuries. In this art form, designs are carved into flat blocks of wood or, to make intricate prints, into blocks of wood covered with linoleum. There is a separate block for each color.

You can use the flat surface of a slice of potato to make a simple block print design to decorate fabric, notepaper, gift wrap, or gift tags.

Potatoes are easy to carve with a pocketknife or paring knife. One large russet potato will provide two slices suitable for making prints. You can make a pattern on construction paper or a 3-by-5-inch card or carve a freehand design directly into the potato slice. Simple designs are the most effective. (Adult supervision is necessary for this project.)

Materials
Old newspapers
Several large russet potatoes
Paring knife or pocketknife
Construction paper or 3-by-5 inch cards for patterns
Pencil
Small pie tin or flat saucer
Tempera or acrylic paint
Brush, 1 or 2 inches wide
Continuous roll of white shelf paper or 18 by-24-inch plain newsprint paper (for gift wrap), unlined 3-by-5-inch cards (for gift tags), notepaper, or fabric
Scissors
Yarn

Step 1.
Cover your work surface with old newspapers.

Step 2.
Cut a potato in half. The cut surface should be evenly flat.

Step 3.
Place the cut end on a 3-by-5-inch card or a scrap of construction paper and draw around the circumference with a pencil. Draw a design to fit inside this penciled shape. (See samples next page.)

Step 4.
Cut out the pattern.

Step 5.
Place the pattern over the cut side of the potato. Use a knife to trace the design to a depth of about ¼ inch. The edges of the design should be cleanly cut.

Step 6.

Pour some paint into the pie tin or saucer. Use the brush to smooth it out.

Step 7.

Press the cut side of the potato in the paint. Use the brush to evenly distribute the paint on all raised surfaces of the design and to remove excess paint.

Step 8.

Using even pressure, stamp the design onto the paper or fabric. If you are making gift tags, leave a space to punch a hole. Repeat the process until you have decorated the item to your satisfaction. Allow the paint to dry thoroughly.

Step 9.

For gift tags, thread yarn through the holes to attach to the gifts.

63. Fruit- and Vegetable-Printed Gift Wrap

Cut an apple, orange, or lemon in half, and you will discover that each fruit has a unique pattern. Vegetables, especially bell pepper and mushroom halves, also have attractive patterns. Use these halves as stamps to create gift-wrapping paper with tempera or poster paint. To add variety to your paper, use more than one color or several kinds of fruits or vegetables.

You can also use the fruit and vegetable stamps to make tags that coordinate with your wrapping paper. Print unlined index cards and add colorful yarn or ribbon in a matching color. Fruit and vegetable prints can be framed and hung on the wall, too.

Materials

Old newspapers

Continuous roll of white shelf paper or 18-by-24-inch sheets of plain newsprint paper

Tempera or poster paint

Paper plates or aluminum pie tins

Brush, 1 or 2 inches wide

Fruits and vegetables (oranges, lemons, limes, apples, bell peppers, mushrooms)

Step 1.
Cover your work surface with old newspapers.

Step 2.
Pour tempera or poster paint into paper plates or pie tins and smooth it with the brush. Make sure it is not lumpy.

Step 3.
Cut fruits and vegetables in half—apples and mushrooms from end to end, and citrus fruits and bell peppers across the width.

Step 4.
Dip the cut edge of the fruit into the paint. Use the brush to distribute the paint evenly over the surface of the fruit. Shake off any excess paint.

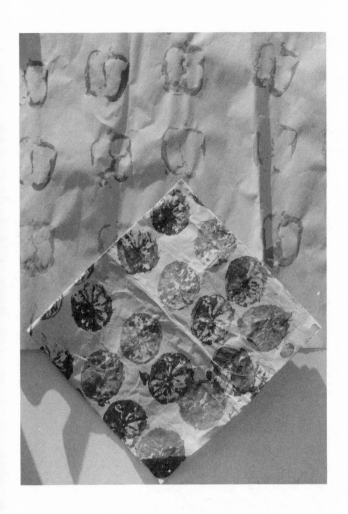

Step 5.

Press the fruit onto the paper. Stamp evenly, applying even pressure. To avoid smears, do not wiggle the fruit. Lift the fruit or vegetable from the paper. You can make several prints from each application of paint. Repeat the process until you have covered the surface of the paper to your satisfaction.

Step 6.

Place the completed paper where the paint can dry. If you have a clothesline, use clothespins to hang the prints up to dry.

64. Herbal or Fruit-Flavored Vinegar

Flavored vinegars make wonderful, inexpensive gifts. They are simple to use and to store. Fruit vinegars keep for about four months at room temperature. Herbal vinegars last longer.

Fruit vinegars can be sprinkled on cooked vegetables, drizzled on fruit salad, or used as a marinade for meat, poultry, or fish. Berry vinegars are excellent marinades for poultry and lamb. Herbal vinegars make tasty salad dressings and can also be used to improve the flavor of cooked vegetables.

Save empty glass salad dressing bottles or other bottles with interesting shapes to use as containers.

Materials

    White, cider, or wine vinegar
    Glass bottles
    2- to 3-cup pan
    2-cup measuring cup
    Tongs
    Flavorings (fruit or herbs and honey)
    Pot holder
    Strainer
    Bowl
    Funnel (optional)

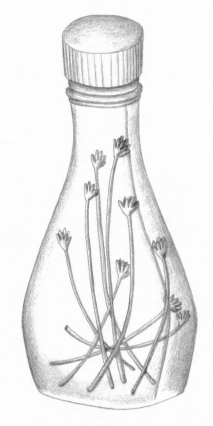

Fruit Vinegar

2 cups white vinegar
Raspberries or blueberries, washed
1 tablespoon honey

Sterilize the bottle and cap by boiling them for about 5 minutes. Carefully lift them from the boiling water with tongs. Using a pot holder, drain any water from the bottle. Pour the water out of the pan and add the vinegar, fruit, and honey. Cover the pan and bring just to a boil. Remove it from the heat and allow the vinegar to stand, covered, until it is cool. For a stronger fruit flavor, allow the vinegar to stand in a cool place for 3 days before straining. Then strain the vinegar to remove fruit and pour into the sterilized bottle, using a funnel if necessary. If you wish, you can add ¼ cup of additional washed fresh fruit to the vinegar. Cap the bottle and allow the vinegar to stand a day before using.

This recipe makes two 8-ounce bottles or one 16-ounce bottle of vinegar.

Herbal Vinegar

2 cups white or cider vinegar
Fresh basil, dill, lavender, tarragon, or rosemary

Sterilize the bottle and cap, following the directions in the recipe for fruit vinegar. Wash herbs and pack them into the bottle. Measure the vinegar into a pan and bring just to a boil. Cool slightly. Pour it into the bottle, using a funnel if necessary. Cap and allow the flavors to penetrate the vinegar for about two weeks before using. It is not necessary to remove the herbs.

65. Natural Ink

Long ago, people had to rely on juice from beets, fruits, spices, and berries for ink and dyes. Today, although these products are now commercially produced, it is still fun to experiment with colorful inks made from natural products.

For red ink, use juice from beets, berries, or red plums. Soak cloves and allspice to produce a scented brown ink. Children will enjoy writing notes with onion juice ink, which is invisible. The writing appears when the paper is ironed.

Here are instructions for four types of natural ink. Experiment with other varieties. Inks made from fruits should be stored in the refrigerator.

Fruit Ink

Materials

1 cup packed red fruit, such as plums or berries

¼ cup boiling or very hot water

2 small bowls

Tablespoon

Strainer

Small bottles

Small funnel

Paper towels or cheesecloth

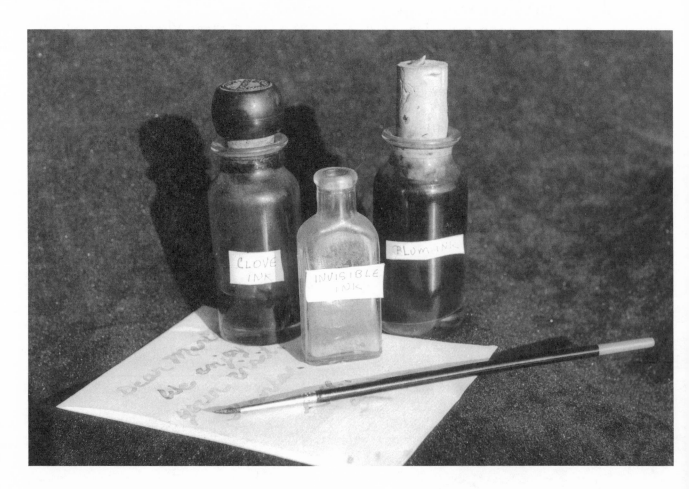

Step 1.
Remove any pits from the fruit. Chop the fruit and pack it into a bowl.

Step 2.
Pour ¼ cup boiling or very hot water over the fruit.

Step 3.
Mash the fruit with a spoon to extract the juices. Pour the juice through a strainer into a second small bowl.

Step 4.
Line the funnel with paper towels or cheesecloth and place it in the mouth of a small bottle.

Step 5.
Pour the juice through the lined funnel, which will strain out fine bits of pulp and peel.

Clove or Allspice Aromatic Ink

Materials
    ¼ cup whole cloves, allspice, or both
    2 small bowls
    Boiling water
    Strainer
    Small funnel
    Paper towels or cheesecloth
    Small bottle

Step 1.
Place cloves and or allspice in small bowl, and just cover with boiling water. Allow the mixture to set several hours or overnight.

Step 2.
Pour the mixture through the strainer into a second small bowl to remove the spices.

Step 3.
Line a small funnel with paper towels or cheesecloth and place it in the mouth of a small bottle.

Step 4.
Strain the liquid from the spices through the funnel. This ink can be kept at room temperature.

Invisible Onion Ink

Materials
    Medium yellow onion
    Garlic press
    Knife
    Measuring cup
    Small jar
    Small watercolor brush
    Paper
    Iron

Step 1.
Cut the onion into small pieces. Press them through a garlic press to extract the juice. Pour

the juice into a measuring cup. Clean the fibers out of the press frequently so that it won't get clogged up.

Step 2.

Pour the juice into a small bottle.

Step 3.

Write a message on paper with the onion ink, using a small brush. The writing will be invisible. Allow the onion juice to dry.

Step 4.

Heat an iron to the medium setting. Iron the paper, and the message will magically appear. Adult supervision is necessary for this step.

Magenta Beet Ink

Materials
   1 beet
   ½ cup water
   Pan
   Knife
   Small bottle

Step 1.

Cut the beet into two or three pieces and place it in a pan with ½ cup water. Bring the water to a boil, then reduce the heat to a simmer.

Step 2.

When the beet is tender, turn off the heat and let the beet and the juice cool.

Step 3.

Pour off the juice into a small bottle. Use a fine brush to write with this beet ink.

Sand, Seashell, Stones, and Crystals

To see a world in a grain of sand
And a heaven in a wild flower,
Hold Infinity in the palm of your hand
And Eternity in an hour.

—William Blake

Sand, shells, stones, and crystals are wonderful gifts from nature.

Stones can be found almost everywhere on earth and come in many sizes and shapes. Look for smooth, water-tumbled stones near the ocean or on riverbanks. Geodes are rough, plain-looking stones on the outside, but when cut open they reveal a secret treasure of crystals. Crystals have many surfaces that reflect light and are valued for their beauty and mystique.

Sand is made of bits of rocks and shells that have been ground to a fine, powdery consistency. It can be found at the seashore or in deserts. Shells were once the home of sea creatures. They come in a wide variety of delicate colors and surface textures.

66. Sand-Cast Candle

S and-cast candles have a rustic quality because a small amount of sand clings to the surface of the candle. An impression in damp sand serves as a mold. The instructions here call for pressing a glass or jar into the sand to produce a geometric candle, but you can also use your hands to make an irregular impression in the sand and produce a free-form candle. A small votive candle placed in the center of the cavity serves as a wick.

Candlemaking requires melting paraffin in a coffee can or other metal container that is placed in a pan of water. Do not leave the stove unattended, because wax can easily ignite. (Children must be closely supervised.)

Materials

Old newspapers
Shoebox
Sand
1 cup water
5-inch high drinking glass or jar with rounded bottom (optional)
2-inch-high votive candle
Empty coffee can
2 slabs paraffin
Pan of water
Crayon
Stirring stick
Pot holders

Step 1.

Place the shoebox outdoors on several layers of newspaper. Fill the box to the top with sand. Dampen the sand with 1 cup of water. The sand should be uniformly moist but not squishy.

Step 2.

Press the drinking glass or jar into the damp sand to make an impression about 3 inches deep. Remove the glass.

Step 3.

Position the votive candle in the center of the impression. The top of this candle should be slightly below the top of the sand.

Step 4.

Place the paraffin in the coffee can and put the can inside a pan containing about 3 inches of water. Bring the water to a boil on the stove. Do not leave the stove unattended.

Step 5.

When the paraffin has melted, add an old crayon, minus the paper wrapping, for color. Stir with a stick.

Step 6.

Carry the pan of water and paraffin outside to the shoebox. Using pot holders, carefully lift the coffee can from the water. An adult should do this step and the next one.

Step 7.

Pour the liquid paraffin into the mold around the votive candle. The paraffin should just cover the top of the votive candle; the wick must extend above the surface of the paraffin.

Step 8.

Let the candle cool completely before lifting it from the mold. Dust off loose sand from the candle, allowing some sand to remain.

67. Sand-Cast Sea Sculpture

On a visit to the beach, collect seashells, small pieces of glass worn by the motion of the ocean, and bits of driftwood. Also bring home a bucket of sand.

When you get home, you can make a sea sculpture using your finds, sand, and plaster of paris. Display the sculpture in your garden, patio, or room as a reminder of the fun you had at the seashore.

The pictured sculpture ¾ to 1 inch thick. The ideal thickness is ½ to ¾ inch.

Materials

Bucket of sand
Coffee can or plastic container
3 cups water
Plaster of paris, 1-pound box
Measuring cup
Stirring stick
Little seashells and other small beach treasures
Pencil or dowel
Yarn or heavy twine, 8 inches long
Scissors

Step 1.

Moisten sand with 1 or 2 cups water. The sand should be damp but not squishy.

Step 2.

Use your hands to make a cavity the size you want your sculpture.

Step 3.

Pour ½ cup water into the can or other container. Add ½ pound plaster of paris and stir. The plaster should be the consistency of thick pancake batter. Use the plaster within twenty minutes, as it will begin to harden.

Step 4.

Pour the plaster of paris mixture into the cavity. Smooth the surface with your hands. Arrange your beach treasures on the surface, pressing them into the plaster to secure them.

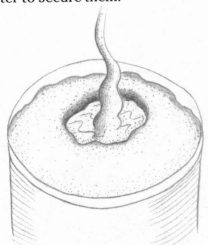

Step 5.

To make a hole for hanging your sculpture, poke a pencil or dowel about ½ inch below the top. Leave it in the hole until the plaster has hardened, occasionally jiggling it so that it won't get stuck in the plaster.

Step 6.

Wait at least an hour before lifting the sculpture out of the sand. Remove the pencil or dowel, and dust loose sand from the back. Cut a piece of yarn or heavy twine and thread it through the hole. Knot the ends of the twine. Hang your sculpture from a hook or nail.

68. Seashell Barrette

Show off assorted small seashells that you collect at the beach or purchase in a craft shop by using them to decorate a barrette for your hair. The size of your barrette will determine how many shells you will need. The barrette in the photo uses about ½ ounce of small seashells.

Materials

Miniature seashells
Plain barrette with a flat surface
Velvet ribbon wide enough to cover the barrette and 3 to 4 inches long
White glue
Scissors

Step 1.

Cut a strip of velvet ribbon the exact length of the barrette. Glue it in place on barrette's top surface with white glue and allow it to dry.

Step 2.

Glue shells to the ribbon, arranging them closely together but leaving a little of the ribbon showing. Allow the glue to dry thoroughly.

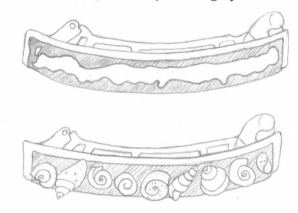

69. Seashell Treasure Box

In the past, visitors to the seashore would often return home with a box or picture frame decorated with seashells as a memento of a summer at the beach. You can easily make one of these treasures by decorating a box with seashells. An inexpensive picture frame with flat surfaces may be decorated in a similar way.

Materials

Small, round wooden Shaker-type box, 3 to 4 inches in diameter, or any small cardboard or wooden box

Small and medium seashells

White glue

Step 1.

Lay out an assortment of seashells. Choose one or two larger shells and glue them to the lid of the box.

Step 2.

Glue small shells to fill in the remaining spaces on the lid. You also may glue smaller seashells on top of the larger shells, but allow some of the larger shell to show. Allow the glue to dry thoroughly.

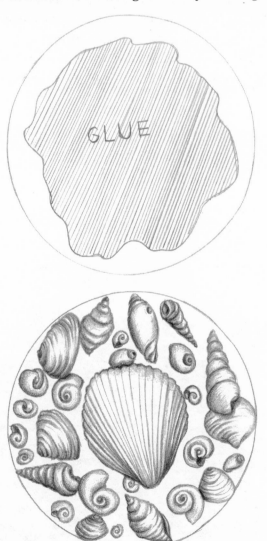

70. Geode Sculpture

Geodes are round stones whose inner cavity is lined with crystals or layers of silica. When geode is cut in half with special lapidary tools, the halves may show a design or pattern. Polished geode halves and slices can be purchased at museums, mineral shops, and rock and gem shows.

This holder made from brass wire turns a geode half or slice into a sculpture. Slices of agate or other stones may also be displayed this way. If the slice of stone is translucent, light can pass through, giving a stained-glass effect.

The size of the geode will determine how much wire you will need. The materials listed here will make a holder for a geode that measures 2½ by 3½ inches. For a larger or heavier geode, use more wire. You can always trim away excess.

Materials

   Geode half or slice
   16-gauge brass wire, 48 to 50 inches long
   24- to 26-gauge thin brass wire
   Ruler
   Needle-nose pliers
   Wire cutter or heavy scissors
   Clear varnish or lacquer (optional)

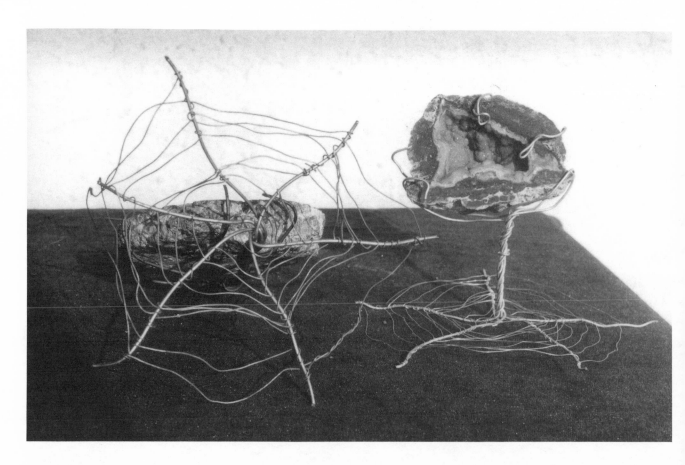

Step 1.
From the 16-gauge brass wire, cut four pieces 9 inches long and one piece 10 inches long.

Step 2.
Arrange the wires so that the 10-inch piece is in the middle, with two shorter wires on each side.

Step 3.
About 3 inches above the bottom ends of the wires, begin twisting the strands together to form a stem. Twist the wires for about 2 inches.

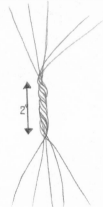

Step 4.
Spread the ends of the wire below the stem out like spokes to form a base for the sculpture to stand on.

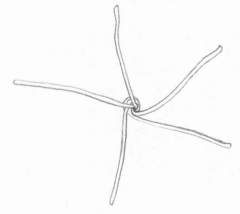

Step 5.
Starting close to the base, anchor the end of the thin wire by twisting it several times around one spoke. Weave around the base, twisting it over and under each spoke. Continue until you have woven the wire around the base to the ends of the spokes. Cut the thin wire, leaving about 1 inch at the end; twist this around the final spoke to anchor the wire web. If you do not want the brass to tarnish, paint or spray it with lacquer or varnish at this point. Allow it to dry.

Step 6.
Spread out the wires above the stem to make a cage or nest to hold the geode. The longest wire should be at the back of the geode. Use needle-nose pliers to loop the end of each wire to hold the geode in place. If the wires seem too long, adjust by clipping the ends. Rest the geode in the holder, tighten the prongs to hold it in place, and adjust the balance by bending the wires at the base so that the sculpture will stand on a table.

71. Fimo Pin with Tumbled Stone

Tumbled gemstones, crystals, and other rocks can be purchased inexpensively at museums, craft shops, and gem stores. If you are lucky, you may find a smooth agate or quartz pebble that has been tossed and smoothed in the ocean. Because of their unusual shapes, making these stones into jewelry has often been difficult. But now, using Fimo, a new modeling material from Germany, these gems can easily be made into unique pieces of jewelry, such as those in the next two projects.

Fimo can be purchased at craft-supply stores. This material comes in many colors. A small block will make several pieces of jewelry.

The material is rolled out and modeled around the stones as mountings. You can press small leaves into rolled-out Fimo, then cut around the leaves and apply onto the setting. There is also Fimo gold and silver powder, which can be dusted onto the material for a metallic finish. Pin backs, available at jewelry-supply stores and some craft stores, are pressed into the back of the mounting before the jewelry is fired. To make a pendant, roll a small piece of Fimo into a loop and apply to the top of the jewelry. The completed objects are hardened by firing in a kitchen oven at a low temperature.

Children age eight and older can use Fimo with supervision.

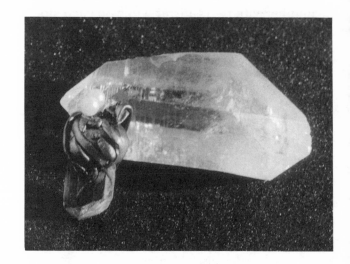

Materials

   1 block Fimo (2 inches square)
   1 small container Fimo gold or silver powder
   Smooth stones
   Small leaves (up to ½ inch long)
   Typing paper
   Jewelry pin back
   Rolling pin or block print roller
   X-acto knife or small paring knife
   Cookie sheet
   Small watercolor brush
   Pot holder
   Cotton swab
   Nail polish remover

Step 1.

Place a sheet of typing paper on a smooth surface. Pinch off a walnut-shell-sized piece of Fimo from the block. Warm it in your hands and roll it into a coil. Use the roller to press the Fimo into a small sheet that has a uniform thickness of about ⅛ inch. The piece must be large enough to wrap the edges of the stone to secure it to the mounting.

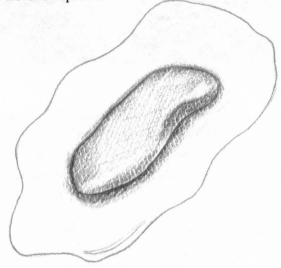

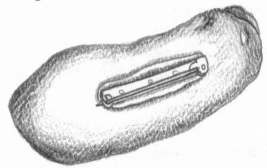

in your hands to make a thin stem. Connect the leaves with the stem, pressing gently with the point of the knife.

Step 2.
Place the stone on the rolled-out Fimo. Use an X-acto knife or paring knife to cut the Fimo around the stone, leaving an extra ¼ to ½ inch all around. Press the edges of the Fimo up around the stone to hold it in place.

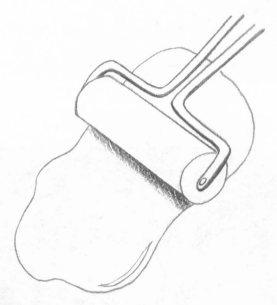

Step 3.
Roll a marble-sized piece of Fimo into a small, thin sheet. Press several small leaves into the sheet to make an impression. Cut around the leaves and remove them carefully. Using the tip of the knife, lift the Fimo leaves and apply them to the surface of the stone, touching the edges of the mounting. Take a small piece of Fimo and roll it

Step 4.
Turn the stone over. Make a roll of Fimo the length of the pin back finding. Press it onto the pin back, then attach this assembly to the back of the stone by pressing the roll against the back of the mounting.

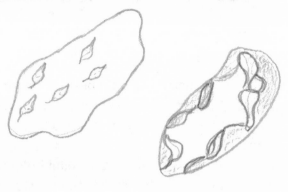

Step 5.
Use the watercolor brush to apply gold or silver powder to the mounting. Try not to get dust on the stone.

Step 6.
Heat the oven to 260° F. Place the pin on a piece of aluminum foil on a cookie sheet and bake for twenty-five minutes. Do not overbake. Remove the cookie sheet from the oven. Allow the pin to cool thoroughly.

Step 7.
Use a cotton swab dipped in nail polish remover to remove any excess metallic dust.

72. Crystal Pendant

Crystals, with their faceted shapes, are favorite stones for jewelry. You can purchase amethyst and quartz crystals in mineral stores and some museum shops.

Using Fimo, it easy to make a pendant holding a small crystal. The rough end of the crystal is encased with Fimo, and a loop at the top enables you to suspend it on a cord or chain.

Materials

Typing paper
Fimo
Pinch of Fimo gold or silver powder
Small crystal, 1 to 2 inches long
Small leaves ¼ to ½ inch long
Paring knife or X-acto knife
Rolling pin or block print roller
Cookie sheet
Pot holder
Cotton swab
Nail polish remover
Chain or cord

Step 1.

Place a piece of clean typing paper on a smooth surface. Pinch off a walnut-shell-sized piece of Fimo from the block. Warm it in your hands to soften it. Use the rolling pin to roll it out to a thickness of about ⅛ inch. Cut off a piece to make cap over the top of the crystal.

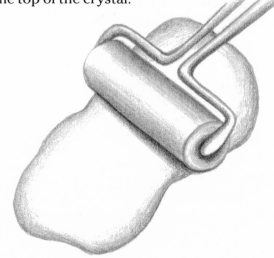

Step 2.

Press Fimo around the top of the crystal. Trim away any excess.

Step 3.

Cut another small piece of Fimo from the sheet and use your hands to make a loop for hanging the crystal from a chain or cord. Stick the loop on the top of the crystal at the back.

Step 4.

Roll out a small amount of Fimo. Press small leaves in the material and cut around them with a paring knife or X-acto knife.

Step 5.

Decorate the top of the crystal with the small cutout leaves and add thin rolls of Fimo to look like stems.

Step 6.

If you want a metallic finish, brush the Fimo with gold or silver dust, taking care not to get the powder on the crystal.

Step 7.

Place the pendant on a cookie sheet and place it in a preheated oven set at 260° F. Bake for 25 minutes. Remove the cookie sheet from the oven. Allow the pendant to cool before you touch it.

Step 8.

Remove any excess metallic dust with a cotton swab saturated with nail polish remover.

Step 9.

Hang the pendant from a chain or cord.